Theodore Gill

Arrangement of the Families of Fishes or Classes Pisces,

Marsipobranchii and Leptocardii

Theodore Gill

Arrangement of the Families of Fishes or Classes Pisces, Marsipobranchii and Leptocardii

ISBN/EAN: 9783741144806

Manufactured in Europe, USA, Canada, Australia, Japa

Cover: Foto ©Thomas Meinert / pixelio.de

Manufactured and distributed by brebook publishing software (www.brebook.com)

Theodore Gill

Arrangement of the Families of Fishes or Classes Pisces, Marsipobranchii and Leptocardii

SMITHSONIAN MISCELLANEOUS COLLECTIONS.

247

ARRANGEMENT

OF THE

FAMILIES OF FISHES,

OR

CLASSES PISCES, MARSIPOBRANCHII, AND LEPTOCARDII.

PREPARED FOR THE SMITHSONIAN INSTITUTION

BY

THEODORE GILL, M.D., Ph.D.

WASHINGTON:
PUBLISHED BY THE SMITHSONIAN INSTITUTION.
NOVEMBER, 1872.

ADVERTISEMENT.

The following list of families of Fishes has been prepared by Dr. Theodore Gill, at the request of the Smithsonian Institution, to serve as a basis for the arrangement of the collection of Fishes of the National Museum; and, as frequent applications for such a list have been received by the Institution, it has been thought advisable to publish it for more extended use. In provisionally adopting this system for the purpose mentioned, the Institution is not to be considered as committed to it, nor as accountable for any of the hypothetical views upon which it may be based.

JOSEPH HENRY,
Secretary, S. I.

Smithsonian Institution,
Washington, October, 1872.

CONTENTS.

INTRODUCTION.

OBJECTS.

A LIST of the families of fishes having long been urgently needed for the re-arrangement of the extensive collections of those animals in the Smithsonian Institution, the following has been drawn up. The author has long delayed its publication in order to continue his investigations and extend them into some more of the many doubtful questions that still involve ichthyology, but as such considerations would cause an indefinite postponement of publication, and as the list itself is desirable as a starting-point for renewed investigation, and is, of course, more available in a printed form than in manuscript, it is now printed; being printed, its publication has been deemed advisable as it may supply to others the want that has been experienced by the Smithsonian Institution. That it will stand the test of time as to many details is not to be expected.

STATUS OF ICHTHYOLOGY.

Studies in ichthyology have, for the most part, been directed to the external organization, and the characters of all but the highest groups have been chiefly derived from features visible from the exterior, and modifications of single organs whose co-ordinations with other modifications, and consequently taxonomic values, have not been verified. If a system among fishes thus established has proved to be more true to nature than analogous ones would be among the mammals, birds, or reptiles, it is because so many of the elements of the skeleton, such as the jaws, opercular bones, suborbitals, scapulars, branchiostegal bones, and rays are more or less exposed to view, and the modifications more or less noted, or, when concealed, the contrast taken cognizance of. A classification based on superficial features in the fishes is thus, to a considerable degree, the expression of skeletal modifications, which are themselves the co-ordinates, as experience has shown, of others. For though the characters derived therefrom may not always be actually taken cognizance of in the diagnoses of the groups, they more or less influence the adoption of groups characterized by modifications of such parts. But it is only within certain limits that these modifications are indicative of affinity; often, for example, only recalling ordinal relations determined by the number of the bones and their development. If, in many other cases, the nearer relations of forms have been correctly inferred, it is rather from the tact which practice confers on the student and the suggestions furnished by modifications which may be of slight moment apparently, but which, on account of eccentricity or other cause, strike the observer and often yield true clews to affinities. It is logically, although the premises might be strenuously disavowed, the result of a quasi-adoption of the doctrine of evolution, and the assumption that certain characteristics peculiar to and common (but perhaps only in part) to certain forms, especially when non-adaptive, are indicative of community of origin, and therefore of immediate affinity. Such combinations are often indefinable at first, but are frequently justified finally on a complete study of the anatomy. But those combinations, when not definable, cannot be considered as established, and are deservedly open to suspicion. The author for many years has been collecting the skeletons and especially the skulls of fishes, and their study has assured him of the affinities of many forms whose relations would otherwise have been very doubtful. He has meanwhile been anticipated in the announcement of certain of the results of his studies by Prof. Cope, who has been fortunate in being able to avail himself of the largest collection of skeletons of fishes known to exist.

CLASSIFICATION.

At a future time the views of the author respecting the principles of classification and their application to the fishes will be published in detail.

At present, it need only be stated that he entirely concurs with Prof. Cope in the view that under the general term " Fishes," three perfectly distinct classes (PISCES, MARSIPOBRANCHII, and LEPTOCARDII) are confounded, and he is inclined to agree with Prof. Häckel in the recognition of even wider and certainly more obvious gaps between the typical fishes and the two inferior classes than between any other contiguous classes of vertebrates, but he cannot, with the latter naturalist, admit the title of the Dipnoi to classical rank. As he urged in 1861,[1] the Dipnoi and Polypteridæ (Crossopterygia, Huxley) exhibit so many characters in common that they cannot be very widely separated, and are not even entitled to subclassical distinction.

[1] Gill (Theodore Nicholas). Catalogue of the Fishes of the Eastern Coast of North America, ... [Philadelphia, The Academy of Natural Sciences, 1861,] pp. 12–20.

CLASSES.

The classes thus recognized may be distinguished as follows, the characters used, however, being supplemented by many others:—

I. Skull more or less developed, with the notochord not continued forwards beyond the pituitary body. Brain differentiated and distinctly developed. Heart developed and divided at least into an auricle and ventricle.

   A. Skull well developed, and with a lower jaw. Paired fins developed (sometimes absent through atrophy); and with a shoulder girdle[1] (lyriform or furcula-shaped, curved forwards and with its respective sides connected below[2]), and with pelvic elements. Gills not purse-shaped.

   PISCES.

   B. Skull imperfectly developed and with no lower jaw. Paired fins undeveloped, with no shoulder girdle nor pelvic elements. Gills purse-shaped.

   MARSIPOBRANCHII.

II. Skull undeveloped, with the notochord persistent and extending to the anterior end of the head. Brain not distinctly differentiated. Heart none.

   LEPTOCARDII.

SUBCLASSES OF PISCES.

The most diverse views have been urged within the last few years in regard to the combination into major groups or subclasses of the orders of the true fishes, Profs. Kner,[3] Owen,[4] Lütken,[5] and Cope[6] on the one hand combining the Teleosts and Ganoids into one group or more closely ap-

---

[1] The shoulder girdle of the Elasmobranchiates appears to be homologous with the parazonal or coracoid elements (*vide postea*) of the specialized fishes, the proscapula of the latter having been apparently first developed by exostosis in the Ganoids, and finally become preponderant while the parazonal became proportionately reduced.

[2] This character distinguishes the class Pisces from the Batrachia.

[3] KNER (Rudolph). Batrachiungen über die Ganoiden, als natürliche Ordnung. . . . . < Sitzungsberichte der Kaiserlichen Akademie der Wissenschaften.— Mathematisch—Naturwissenschaftliche Classe, b. 54, 1. abth., 1866, pp. 519-536.

Prof. Kner concludes with the expression of belief that the Ganoids do not form a homogeneous group, and should not, therefore, be retained in the system, and that, far from being an improvement, the introduction of the group was a hindrance to the progress of ichthyology.

[4] OWEN (Richard). On the Anatomy of Vertebrates, v. I, 1860, p. 7; also, v. III, 1868, p. 354 (Zoological Index).

The fishes (Pisces) are divided (in v. I.) into (1) Subclass I. Dermopteri (including Pharyngobranchii and Marsipobranchii); (2) Subclass II. Teleostomi; (3) Subclass III. Plagiostomi; (4) Subclass IV. Dipnoa: Subclass V. Monopnoa is equivalent to the class Batrachia elsewhere (p. 6) admitted by him.

In the Zoological Index, the author reverses the sequence, and designates the "Dipnoi" as a simple order (order *Protopteri*), placing it at the head of the class Pisces.

[5] LÜTKEN (Christian). Prof. Kner on the Classification of the Ganoids. . . . . < The Geological Magazine (London), v. 5, 1869.

proximating them, while, on the other hand, Dr. Günther[a] has contended for the union of the Ganoids, Dipnoans, and Elasmobranchiates into one subclass, for which he has proposed the name PALAEICHTHYES.

———— On Ganoidernes Begrændsning og Inddeling, ... < Videnskabelige Meddelelser fra den naturhistoriske Forening i Kjöbenhavn, for Aaret 1868, 1869, pp. 1-52.

———— On the limits and classification of the Ganoids. . . . . < Annals and Magazine of Natural History, (London), 4th series, v. 7, 1871, pp. 329-339.

Dr. Lütken attaches primary importance to (1) the freedom or attachment of the gills, and (2) the communication of the air bladder with the intestinal canal or exclusion therefrom.

He subordinates the subdivisions as follows:—

Subclass A. TELEOSTEI, ELEUTHEROBRANCHII.
  Order 1. *Physoclisti* s. *Acanthopteri.*
  Order 2. *Physostomi* s. *Malacopteri.*
    Suborder *a.* Typici (including Cycloganoidei).
    Suborder *b.* Ganoidei.
    Suborder *c.* Sturiones.
    Suborder *d.* Protopteri.
Subclass B. CHONDROSTEI s. DERMOBRANCHII.
  Order 3. *Selachii.*
  Order 4. *Cyclostomi.*
  Order 5. *Branchiostomi.*

Incertae sedis.

  Order 6. *Placodermi.*

The above subclass Teleostei is equivalent to the order Branchiata of Pallas, and the subclass Teleostomi of Owen; the subclass Chondrostei, to the class Ichthyulera of Geoffroy St. Hilaire, the order Spiraculata of Pallas, and the order Placoidei of Agassiz.

[1] COPE (Edward Drinker). Observations on the Systematic relations of the Fishes, ... < The American Naturalist (Salem), v. 5, 1871, pp. 579-593; also, (somewhat modified) < Proceedings of the American Association for the Advancement of Science, 1871 (1872), pp. 317-343.

Prof. Cope's primary divisions or subclasses of the class Pisces are as follows:—

Subclass HOLOCEPHALI.
Subclass SELACHII.
Subclass DIPNOI.
Subclass CROSSOPTERYGII.
Subclass ACTINOPTERI.
  Tribe *Chondrostei.*
  Tribe *Physostomi.*
    Order Ginglymodi (*Lepidosteidae*).
    Order Halecomorphi (*Amiidae*).

The succeeding orders of Physostomi and the Physoclysti are all Teleosteans of Müller.

[1] GÜNTHER (Albert C. L. G.). The new Ganoid fish (Ceratodus) recently discovered in Queensland. < Nature, (London,) v. 4, 1871, pp. 406-408, 428-429, (447).

The author, after a careful review of the subject, is compelled to agree with Messrs. Kner, Owen, Lütken, and Cope in the closer combination of the Teleosts, Ganoids, and Dipnoans and the contradistinction of the united group from the Elasmobranchiates, and is even disposed to admit that the range of variation in the Ganoid series is so great that less difference appears to exist between the most teleosteoid Ganoids (e. g., *Amia*) and the Teleosteans than between them and the most generalised Ganoids (e. g., *Polypterus* and *Acipenser*). But, notwithstanding this, the establishment by Johannes Müller of the subclass for which he adopted the name Ganoidei appears to have been one of the most important in the history of Ichthyology, as it was the expression of the discovery of characters which undoubtedly indicate affinity, and, however much recent Ichthyologists have dissented from him as to the boundaries of groups, all have left the Ganoids in immediate juxtaposition to each other, and have chiefly differed from him as to the point where the primary division should be established, whether on one side or other of the Müllerian Ganoids.

In the following list of families, the three subclasses of true fishes established by Müller are still retained, but are combined under two series, TELEOSTOMI (Owen) and ELASMOBRANCHII (Bon., Müll.), and the several superorders are distinguished among the Ganoids. For while the author is prepared to admit that the extremes of the Ganoids are more dissimilar than one of those extremes and the typical physostome Teleosts, it is not yet apparent that the relations between the Ganoids and Teleosts are as intimate as those between the contiguous orders of the latter series.

ORDERS OF PISCES.

After a recent review of the various proposals for the modification of the system by various authors, and due examination of the animals themselves, the author is compelled to retain the orders of Teleosts adopted in the classification proposed by him in 1861, suppressing, however, the (then

—— Description of Ceratodus, a genus of Ganoid Fishes, recently discovered in rivers of Queensland, Australia. . . . . < Philosophical Transactions of the Royal Society of London, v. 161, 1872, pp. 511-571, pl. 30-42.

Dr. Günther recognizes only two orders among Palæichthyes, viz:—

Fourth subclass: PALÆICHTHYES.
  Order 1. *Chondropterygii.*
    Suborder 1. *Plagiostoma.*
    Suborder 2. *Holocephala.*
  Order 2. *Ganoidei.*
    Suborder 1. *Amioidei.*
    Suborder 2. *Lepidosteoidei.*
    Suborder 3. *Polypteroidei.*
    Suborder 4. *Chondrostei.*
    Suborder 5. *Dipnoi.*

so stated) provisional order Lemniscati (which, as he subsequently urged,[1] was a heterogeneous group based upon the larvae of other fishes but primarily those of *Muraenidae*), and adopting among the Teleost series the orders OPISTHOMI, HEMIBRANCHII, and SCYPHOPHORI (Cope), the last of which was subsequently approximated by the author[a] to the NEMATOGNATHI, a view since confirmed by Prof. Cope.

All the orders thus adopted, so far as considerable material indicate, appear to be well distinguished by peculiarities of the skeleton and the nervous system. The peculiarities of the skeleton are expressed in the skull, (1) especially in the varying combinations of the elements which compose the cranial box, as well as (2) the palato-pterygoid system, and (3) the suspensorium of the lower jaw, while in (4) the modifications of the shoulder girdle, other excellent characters are found. These are to a greater or less extent co-ordinated with and confirmed by (5) the development of the brain, especially the internal structure of the optic lobes and the relations of the various parts. These characters certainly seem to be of more importance than the development of some of the bones that sustain the fins as (*pro*) rays or as (*con*) spines, and as there is no co-ordination between the latter developments and other modifications of structure, the groups so distinguished must be admitted to have a very unsatisfactory basis. And surely it is rather illogical to urge that other characters are of little importance because they do not coincide with the structure of the fin-rays, for the question at issue is taken for granted. But so wedded

---

[1] GILL (Theodore Nicholas). On the Affinities of several doubtful British Fishes, ... < Proceedings of the Academy of Natural Sciences of Philadelphia, 1864, pp. 207-298; *reprinted* (in part). < Annals and Magazine of Natural History, 3d series, v. 15, 1864, p. 4.

Dr. Günther subsequently endorsed these views in general (v. 8, p. 177), but having mistaken the tenor of the remarks of the author, has afterwards stated, in respect to *Stomiasunculus*, that he "cannot agree with Mr. Gill, who compares this fish to a larval Clupeoid" (v. 8, p. 145). It will be evident, however, on reperusal, that I by no means meant to suggest that *Stomiasunculus* had any *affinity* with Clupeoids, the statement being that "*Stomiasunculus* resembles, in *general features*, a less advanced [than *Esocidæ*] Clupeoid, about three days old, in which the ventral fins have not yet appeared." The comparison of the form in question with the larval Clupeoid was evidently simply to verify the probability of the immature condition of *Stomiasunculus*, but the true affinities were sought for elsewhere. It was added, "suspicion, however, may be entertained that it may, perhaps, be the young of some other type (possibly Stomiatoids), on account of the backward position of the dorsal fin." Such is also the opinion of Dr. Günther himself, who remarks that "this is evidently the young of *Stomias* or of a fish very closely allied to it." More than this, the evidence would not authorize.

[a] GILL (Theodore Nicholas). Synopsis of the Fishes of the Gulf of St. Lawrence and Bay of Fundy, ... < The Canadian Naturalist and Geologist (Montreal), 2d series, v. 2, 1864, p. 252.

is the mind generally to impressions early received or which have become current, that insensibly the premises in dispute are assumed and results viewed with preconceptions reflected from the assumed premises.

But at the same time, caution must be exercised lest too great importance is attached to the minor modifications. For example, the great frontal bone in the Gadinae and near related subfamilies is single, as in many other fishes, but in the subfamily Lotinae and in the family Merluciidae, two entirely separate bones exist instead. Again, the inferior pharyngeal bones are generally distinct in the Teleocephali, but in several families they are united more or less early, and, in the extreme forms, very soon, losing all trace of suture, and the eminent Johannes Müller was led to separate the forms so distinguished from other fishes as a distinct order (Pharyngognathi); that such a combination, however, was somewhat hasty is demonstrable, independently of hypothetical considerations as to the values of characters by certain facts. First, the combination thus formed was a heterogeneous one, definable by no other internal or external common characters, and composed of forms which respectively agreed in structure, in all other respects, in the closest manner with other widely separated types, and thus the character became tainted with suspicion. Second, in another form (*Haploidonotus*) agreeing (generically) in almost all details — and very characteristic ones moreover — with forms (Sciaenidae) possessed generally of entirely separated bones, the pharyngeal bones were found united as entirely as, and even more so than, in typical Pharyngognathi of Müller, and it thus became evident that *per se* a combination based on such a character would violently divorce forms from their natural allies, and it was equally evident that the character itself was one liable to recur in very dissimilar groups, and not even having the advantage of being a technical expression of a natural group.

With these remarks, examination may be made of the various orders of fishes that have been adopted, commencing with those forms that appear to be the most generalized or least removed from the Ganoids; the sequence herein adopted is the most convenient for present purposes, and is also believed to be a tolerably close exponent of nature.

But as it will be necessary to make use of some elements concerning which much difference of opinion prevails among anatomists, the author deems it advisable to digress in order to examine into the merits of the questions in dispute, and present his reasons for the nomenclature subsequently adopted.

EXCURSUS ON THE SHOULDER GIRDLE OF FISHES.

Few problems involving the homologies of bones in the vertebrate branch have been in so unsatisfactory a condition as that respecting the shoulder girdle and its constituents in fishes. But the recent observations of Bruhl, Gegenbaur, and Parker have thrown a flood of light upon the subject. Some minor questions, however, appear still to be unsettled; the writer, at least, has not been able to convince himself of the correctness of all the identifications, and of the names conferred as expressions thereof. Recent study has increased such doubts respecting the applicability of former nomenclature, and has led to conclusions different from those announced by previous investigators.

The following are assumed as premises that will be granted by all zootomists :—

1. Homologies of parts are best determinable, *cæteris paribus*,[1] in the most nearly related forms.

2. Identifications should proceed from a central or determinate point outwards.

The applications of these principles are embodied in the following conclusions :—

1. The forms that are best comparable and that are most nearly related to each other, are the Dipnoi, an order of fishes at present represented by *Lepidosiren*, *Protopterus*, and *Ceratodus*, and the Batrachians as represented by the Ganocephala, Salamanders, and Salamander-like animals.

2. The articulation of the anterior member with the shoulder girdle forms the most obvious and determinable point for comparison in the representatives of the respective classes.

THE GIRDLE IN DIPNOANS.

I.

The proximal element of the anterior limb in the Dipnoi has, almost by common consent, been regarded as homologous with the HUMERUS of the higher vertebrates.

II.

The humerus in the Urodele Batrachians, as well as the extinct Ganocephala and Labyrinthodontia, is articulated chiefly with the coracoid.

Therefore, the element of the shoulder girdle with which the humerus of the Dipnoi is articulated, must also be regarded as the CORACOID (subject to the proviso hereinafter stated), unless some specific evidence can be shown to the contrary. No such evidence has been produced.

III.

The scapula in the Urodele and other Batrachians is entirely or almost wholly excluded from the glenoid foramen, and above the coracoid.

Therefore, the corresponding element in Dipnoi must be the SCAPULA.

---

[1] Parts affected by teleological modifications may be excepted.

IV.

The other elements must be determined by their relation to the preceding, or to those parts from or in connection with which they originate.

All those elements in *immediate* connection[1] with the pectoral fin and the scapula must be homologous as a whole with the coraco-scapular plate of the Batrachians,—that is, it is infinitely more probable that they represent as a whole or as dismemberments therefrom the coraco-scapular element than that they have independently originated.

But the homogeneity of that coraco-scapular element forbids the identification of the several elements of the Fishes' shoulder girdle with regions of the Batrachian's coraco-scapular plate.

And it is equally impossible to identify the fishes' elements with those of the higher reptiles or other vertebrates which have developed from the Batrachians. The elements in the shoulder girdles of the distantly separated classes may be (to use the terms introduced by Dr. Lankester) homoplastic, but they *are not* homogenetic.

Therefore, they must be named accordingly.

The element of the Dipnoan's shoulder girdle, continuous downwards from the scapula, and to which the coracoid is closely applied, may be named ECTOCORACOID.

V.

Neither the scapula in Batrachians nor the cartilaginous extension thereof, designated Suprascapula, is dissevered from the coracoid.

Therefore, there is an *à priori* improbability against the homology with the scapula of any part having a distant or merely ligamentous connection with the humerus-bearing element.

Consequently, as an element better representing the scapula exists, the element named scapula (by Owen, Günther, etc.) cannot be the homologue of the scapula of Batrachians.

On the other hand, its more intimate relations with the skull and the mode of development indicate that it is rather an element originating and developed in more intimate connection with the skull.

It may therefore be considered, with Parker, as a POSTTEMPORAL.

VI.

The shoulder girdle in the Dipnoi is connected by an azygous differentiated cartilage, swollen backwards.

It is more probable that this is the homologue of the STERNUM of Batrachians, and that in the latter, that element has been still more differentiated and specialised than that it should have originated *de novo* from an independently developed nucleus.

---

[1] The so scapula and suprascapula of most authors are excluded from this connection.

The homologies of the elements of the shoulder girdle of the Dipnoi appear then to be as follows:—

Nomenclature Adopted.	Owen.	Parker.	Günther.
Humerus.	Humerus.	Humerus.	Forearm.
Coracoid (or Paraglenal).[1]		Scapula.	Humeral cartilage.
Scapula.	Coracoid.	Supraclavicle.	Coracoid.[4]
Ectocoracoid (or Coracoid) [2]		Clavicle.	
Sternum.[3]		Epicoracoid.	Median cartilage.
Posttemporal.	Scapula.	Posttemporal.	Suprascapula.

THE GIRDLE IN OTHER FISHES.

Proceeding from the basis now obtained, a comparative examination of other types of Fishes successively removed by their affinities from the Lepidosirenids may be instituted.

I.

With the humerus of the Dipnoans, the element in the Polypterids (single at the base but immediately divaricating, and with its limbs bordering an intervening cartilage which supports the pectoral and its basilar ossicles) must be homologous.

But it is evident that the external elements of the so-called carpus of teleosteoid Ganoids are homologous with that element in Polypterids.

Therefore, those elements cannot be carpal, but must represent the humerus.

[1] Gelenkstelle der Brustflosse am primären Schulterknorpel.—Gegenbaur.

[2] Clavicula.—Gegenbaur.

[3] Verbindungsstelle des beiderseitigen Schulterknorpels.—Gegenbaur.

Prof. Gegenbaur regards the median cartilage as a dismemberment of a common cartilage, the upper division of which receives the pectoral limb, while the lower unites with the corresponding dismemberment of the opposite side and forms the median cartilage.

[4] The suture separating the "coracoid" into two portions has been observed by Dr. Günther, but he could "not attach much importance to this division."

II.

The element with which the homologue of the humerus, in Polypterids, is articulated must be homologous with the analogous element in Dipnoans, and therefore with the Coracoid.

The Coracoid of Polypterids is also evidently homologous with the corresponding element in the other Ganoids, and the latter consequently must be also Coracoid.

It is equally evident, after a detailed comparison, that the single Coracoid element of the Ganoids represents the three elements developed in the generalized Teleosts (Cyprinids, etc.) In connection with the basis of the pectoral fin, and such being the case, the nomenclature should correspond. Therefore, the upper element may be named Hypercoracoid; the lower, Hypocoracoid; and the transverse or median, Mesocoracoid.

III—IV.

(Proscapula, or united Scapula and Ectocoracoid.)

The two elements of the arch named by Parker, in Lepidosiren, "supraclavicle" (= scapula), and "clavicle" (= ectocoracoid) seem to be comparable together, and as a whole with the single element carrying the humerus and pectoral fin in the Crossopterygians (*Polypterus* and *Calamoichthys*) and other fishes,[1] and therefore not identical respectively with the "supraclavicle" and "clavicle" (except in part) recognized by him in other fishes.

As this compound bone, composed of the scapula and ectocoracoid fused together, has received no name which is not ambiguous or deceptive in its homological allusions, it may be designated as Proscapula.

V.

The posttemporal of the Dipnoans is evidently represented by the analogous element in the Ganoids generally, as well as in the typical fishes.

The succeeding elements (outside those already alluded to) appear from their relations to be developed from or in connection with the posttemporal, and not from the true scapular apparatus; they may therefore be named Posttemporal, Posterotemporal, and Teleotemporal.

---

[1] Dr. Günther (Phil. Trans., v. 161, p. 531) has observed, respecting the division in question in *Lepidosiren* and *Ceratodus*: "I cannot attach much value to this division; the upper piece is certainly not homologous with the scapula of Teleostean fishes, which is far removed from the region of the pectoral condyle."

The homologies of the elements of the girdle of Dipnoans with those of other fishes, and the added elements in the latter will be as follows :—

	Cuvier.	Owen.	Gegenbaur.	Parker.
ACTINOSTE.	Os du carpe.	Carpal.	Basalstücke der Brustflösse.	Brachial.
CORACOID or PARAGLENAL		Simple in Dipnoi and Ganoidei		
HYPERCORACOID.	Radial.	Ulna.	Oberes Stück (Scapulare).	Scapula.
MESOCORACOID.	Troisième os de l'avant bras qui porte l'nageoire pectorale.	Humerus.	Spangenstück.	Procoracoid.
HYPOCORACOID.	Cubital.	Radius.	Vorderes Stück (Procoracoid).	Coracoid.
PROSCAPULA.[1]	Huméral.	Coracoid.	Clavicula.	Clavicle.
SCAPULA. ECTOCORACOID.	}	Differentiated only in Dipnoi.		
STERNUM.		Differentiated in Dipnoi.		
		POSTTEMPORAL ELEMENTS.		
POSTTEMPORAL.	Suprascapulaire.	Suprascapula.	Supraclaviculare (a).	Posttemporal.
POSTSUPRATEMPORAL.	Scapulaire.	Scapula.	Supraclaviculare (b).	Supraclavicle.
TELOSUPRATEMPORAL.	Os coracoidien.	Clavicle.	Acromioticon Stück.	Postclavicle.

It will be thus seen that the determinations here adopted depend mainly (1) on the interpretation of the homologies of the elements with which the pectoral limbs are articulated, and (2) on the application of the term "coracoid." The name "coracoid," originally applied to the process so called in the human scapula, and subsequently extended to the independent element homologous with it in birds and other vertebrates, has been more especially retained (e. g., by Parker in Mammals, etc.) for the region including the glenoid cavity. On the assumption that this may be preferred by most zootomists, the preceding terms have been applied. But, if the name should be restricted to the proximal element, nearest the glenoid cavity, in which ossification commences, the name PARAGLENAL given by

[1] The name scapula might have been retained for this element as it is (if the views here maintained are correct) homologous with the entire scapula of man, less the coracoid and glenoid elements, but the restricted meaning has been so universally adopted that it would be inexpedient now to extend the word.

Doges to the cartilaginous glenoid region can be adopted, and the cora-coid would then be represented (in part), rather by the element so named by Owen. That eminent anatomist, however, reached his conclusion (only in part the same as that here adopted) by an entirely different course of reasoning, and by a process, as it may be called, of elimination; that is, recognizing first the so-called "radius" and "ulna," the "humerus," the "scapula," and the "coracoid" were successively identified from their rela-tions to the elements thus determined, and because they were numerically similar to the homonymous parts in higher vertebrates.

The detailed arguments for these conclusions, and references to the views of other authors, will be given in a future memoir. I will only add here that these homologies seem to be fully sustained by the relations of the parts in the generalized Ganocephalous Batrachians (*Apateon* or *Archego-saurus*, etc.).

CHARACTERISTICS AND SEQUENCE OF PRIMARY GROUPS.

Returning now to the consideration of the primary classification of Fishes, the results are submitted, in brief, of inquiries thus far instituted into the limits, characters, and relations of the orders and including groups.

While among the Mammals, there is almost[1] universal concurrence as to the forms entitled to the first as well as the last places, naturalists differ much concerning the "highest" of the ichthyoid vertebrates, but are all of one accord respecting the form to be designated as the "lowest." With that admitted lowest form as a starting-point, inquiry may be made re-specting the forms which are successively *most nearly related*.

LEPTOCARDIANS.

No dissent has ever been expressed from the proposition that the Lepto-cardians (*Branchiostoma*) are the lowest of the Vertebrates; while they have doubtless deviated much from the representatives of the immediate line of descent of the higher vertebrates, and are probably specialized con-siderably, in some respects, in comparison with those vertebrates from which they (in common with the higher forms) have descended, they un-doubtedly have diverged far less, and furnish a better hint as to the proto-vertebrates than any other form.

MARSIPOBRANCHIATES.

Equally undisputed is it that most nearly related to the Leptocardians

[1] One eminent authority appears to think that the Cetaceans are the lowest and most differentiated of Mammals, and, as a matter of fact, no one, it is presumed, would dispute the proposition that the differences are more obvious, but they are *teleological*, and not *morphological*; therefore, and in view of the gradation between them and normal quadrupeds furnished by extinct types, naturalists are almost agreed in denying the characters in question a taxonomic value equal to that accorded to the differences exhibited by the Monotremes.

are the Marsipobranchiates (*Lampreys*, etc.), and the tendency has been rather to overlook the fundamental differences between the two, and to approximate them too closely, than the reverse.

PISCES.

But here unanimity ends, and much difference of opinion has prevailed with respect to the succession in the system of the several sub-classes (by whatever name called) of true Fishes, (1) some (*e. g.* Cuvier, J. Müller, Owen, Lütken, Cope) arranging next to the lowest, the Elasmobranchiates and, as successive forms, the Ganoids and Teleosteans, (2) while others (*e. g.* Agassiz, Dana, Duméril, Günther) adopt the sequence Leptocardians, Marsipobranchiates, Teleosteans, Ganoids, and Elasmobranchiates. The source of this difference of opinion is evident, and results partly from metaphysical or psychological considerations, and partly from those based (in the case of the Ganoids) on real similarities and affinities.

ELASMOBRANCHIATES.

The evidence in favor of the title of the Elasmobranchiates to the "highest" rank is based upon, (1) the superior development of the brain; (2) the development of the egg, and the ovulation; (3) the possession of a placenta; and (4) the complexity of the organs of generation.

(1) It has not been definitely stated wherein the superior development of the brain consists, and as it is not evident to the author, the vague claim can only be met by this simple statement: it may be added, however, that the brains comparable in essentials and most similar as a whole to those of the Marsipobranchiates, are those of the Sharks. In answer to the statement that the Sharks exhibit superior intelligence, and thus confirm the indications of cerebral structure, it may be replied that the impression is a subjective one, and the author has not been thus influenced by his own observations of their habits. Psychological manifestations, at any rate, furnish too vague criteria to be available in exact taxonomy

(2) If the development of the eggs, their small number, and their investment in cases, are arguments in favor of the high rank of the Elasmobranchiates, they are also for the Marsipobranchiates, and thus prove too much —or too little—for the advocates of the view discussed. The variation in number of progeny among true Fishes (*e. g., Cyprinodonts, Embiotocids*) also demonstrates the unreliability of those modifications *per se.*

(3) The so-called placenta of some Elasmobranchiates may be *analogous* to that of Mammals, but that it is not *homologous* (*i. e.*, homogenetic) is demonstrable from the fact that all the forms intervening between them and the specialized placental mammals are devoid of a placenta, and by the variation (presence or want) among the Elasmobranchiates themselves.

(4) The organs of generation in the Elasmobranchiates are certainly

more complex than in most other Fishes, but as the complexity results from specialization of parts *sui generis*, and different from those of the higher (quadruped) vertebrates, it is not evident what bearing the argument has. If it is claimed simply on the ground of specialization, irrespective of homological agreement with admitted higher forms, then are we equally entitled to claim any specialization of parts as evidence of high rank, or at least we have not been told within what limits we should be confined. The Cetaceans, for example, are excessively specialized Mammals, and, on similar grounds, would rank above the other Mammals and Man; the Aye-aye exhibits in its dentition excessive specialization and deviation from the primitive type (as exhibited in its own milk teeth) of the Primates, and should thus also rank above Man. It is true that in other respects the higher Primates (even excluding man) may be more specialized, but the specialization is not as obvious as in the cases referred to, and it is not evident how we are to balance *irrelative* specializations against each other, or even how we shall subordinate such cases.[1] We are thus compelled by the *reductio ad absurdum* to the confession that *irrelative* specialization of single organs is untrustworthy, and are fain to return to that better method of testing affinities by the equation of agreement in whole, and after the elimination of special teleological modifications.

The question then recurs, What forms are the most *nearly allied* to the Marsipobranchiates, and what show the closest approach in *characteristic* features. And in response thereto, the evidence is not undecisive. Wide as is the gap between Marsipobranchiates and Fishes, and comparatively limited as is the range of the latter among themselves, the Elasmobranchiates are very appreciably more like, and share more characters in common with them, than any other; so much is this the case, that some eminent naturalists (e. g. Pallas, Geoffroy St.-Hilaire, Latreille, Agassiz (formerly), Lütken) have combined the two forms in a peculiar group, contradistinguished from the other fishes. The most earnest and extended argument, in English, in favor of this combination, has been published by Prof. Agassiz, in his "Lake Superior,"[2] but that eminent naturalist subsequently arrived at the opposite conclusions already indicated.

The evidences of the closer affinity of the Elasmobranchiates (than of any other Fishes) with the Marsipobranchiates, are furnished by (1) the cartilaginous condition of the skeleton; (2) the post-cephalic position of the branchiæ; (3) the development of the branchiæ, and their restriction to special chambers; (4) the larger number of branchiæ; (5) the imperfect develop-

---

[1] It will recur to the reader that in the case referred to, the question is really as to the *degree* of specialization.

[2] Agassiz (Louis). Lake Superior: its Physical Character, Vegetation, and Animals. 1850, pp. 249–252.

ment of the skull; (6) the mode of attachment of the teeth; (7) the slight degree of specialization of the rays of the fins; and (8) the rudimentary condition of the shoulder-girdle.

In none of these cases is there exact, or even very close similarity, for, as already remarked, the gap between the Fishes (and the Elasmobranchiates as the most generalized form) and the Marsipobranchiates is extremely wide. In each case, however, the generalized or rudimentary condition of the organs points to the still more generalized, rudimentary, or undeveloped conditions exhibited by the Marsipobranchiates. The testimony of these parts is also concurrent, is reinforced by other resemblances, less obvious but valuable as accumulative, and is not offset by the evidence of other parts (unless *irrelative* specialization of isolated parts is considered as contradictory evidence). And still more, there are no other forms that can be compared with the Marsipobranchiates in even approximately so satisfactory a manner. Therefore, with no hesitation, the sub-class of Elasmobranchiates is placed as the succeeding term in the ichthyological series.

PLAGIOSTOMI.

On the whole, the Sharks appear to be the most generalized of the Elasmobranchiates, and there is little doubt but that the Rays are a more specialized offshoot from the same primitive stock.

HOLOCEPHALI.

More nearly related to the Sharks than to the Rays, but differentiated from representatives of a primitive line of descent, the HOLOCEPHALI claim the next consideration. If, in some respects, they appear to be more nearly related to the Ganoids, the Plagiostomes do in others, and it yet remains to be decided which are the most generalized in essential features. Meanwhile, it seems advisable to preserve the place for the Plagiostomi.

GANOIDEI.

By common consent, the Ganoids immediately succeed the Elasmobranchiates. Before considering the sequence of the forms, a brief inquiry into the constitution of the class may be seasonable.

HISTORICAL NOTE.

The name Ganoides (or Gonio1epedoti) was originally framed by Prof. Agassiz[1] as an ordinal term for fishes having the scales (when present)

---

[1] 1er ordre. Ganoïdes Agass. (Goniolepidoti Agass.). Familles anguleuses, rhomboïdales ou polygones, formées de lames osseuses ou cornées, recouvertes d'émail.—Les familles des Lépidoïdes, des Sauroïdes, des Pycnodontes, des Sclerodermes, des Gymnodontes, des Lophobranches, etc. etc.—Agass. Recherches sur les Poissons fossiles, v. 2 p. 1.

angular and covered with enamel; and, in the group so characterized, were combined the Ganoids of subsequent authors as well as the Teleostean orders Plectognathi, Lophobranchii, and Nematognathi, and (subsequently) the genus *Sudis* (*Arapaima*), the last being regarded as a Coelacanth. The group has not been accepted with these limits or characters.

But the researches of Prof. Johannes Müller, on the anatomy and classification of the fishes, culminated at length in his celebrated memoirs on those fishes for which he retained the ordinal name Ganoidei; those memoirs have left an impression on Ichthyology perhaps more decided than made by any other contributions to the science, and that published *in extenso* will ever be classical; numerous as have been the modifications since introduced into the system, no forms except those recognized by Müller (unless it be Dipnoi) have since been interjected among the Ganoids.

Without premonition in any other form, the results of his studies of the Ganoids were announced to the Royal Academy of Sciences of Berlin in December, 1844,[1] and this communication was supplemented, on the 13th February, 1845, by observations on the bulbus arteriosus, and on the 12th March, 1846, by a more extended memoir, giving the results of subsequent investigations.[2] These were combined, and, with his previous contributions

[1] Müller (Johannes). Über den Bau und die Grenzen der Ganoiden und über das natürliche System der Fische. . . . Gelesen in der Akademie der Wissenschaften, am 13 December, 1844.

Published in abstract in the Monatsberichte der Königlichen Preuss. Akademie der Wissenschaften zu Berlin, 1844, pp. 416–422; in advance < Archiv für Naturgeschichte (Berlin), 11 Jahrg., b. 1, 1845, pp. 91–141; in full (with modifications) < Abhandlungen der Königlichen Akademie der Wissenschaften zu Berlin, 1844 (1846), pp. 117–216, 6 pl.

The memoir, as published in the Archiv für Naturgeschichte, was translated into French, English, and Italian, viz:—

——— Mémoire sur les Ganoïdes et sur la classification naturelle des Poissons. . . . < Annales des Sciences Naturelles, 3ᵉ série, v. 4, 1845, pp. 5–53.

This translation was by Dr. Carl Vogt, and was followed by an original memoir (Quelques observations sur les ganoïdes qui servent à la classification des Poissons Ganoïdes. Par M. C. Vogt, pp. 53–65, pl. 9), detailing especially the results of his examination of *Amia* and first revealing its Ganoid characteristics.

——— On the Structure and Characters of the Ganoidei, and on the natural Classification of Fishes. . . . < Scientific Memoirs, selected from the Transactions of foreign academies of science and learned societies, and from foreign Journals, edited by Richard Taylor, v. 4, 1846, pp. 499–558.

[2] ——— Fernere Bemerkungen über den Bau der Ganoiden, ... < Monatsberichte, etc., 1846, pp. 67–85; also, < Archiv für Naturgeschichte, 1846, 1, pp. 190–206.

——— Further Remarks on the Structure of the Ganoidei, ... < Scientific Memoirs, etc., v. 4, pp. 543–558.

to the knowledge of the natural families of fishes, somewhat modified, and published in the extended memoir which appeared in the Transactions (Abhandlungen) of the Society.

The memoir, as finally published in the Abhandlungen, contained additional details (on pp. 118, 126 to 129, physiological observations on the bulbus arteriosus;[1] pp. 154 to 195, Abschnitt II. über die natürlichen Ordnungen und Familien der Knochenfische[2]); the paragraphs on the Apodes, Esoces, Galaxiæ, and Clupesoces in the Archiv (pp. 131–134) were omitted, and a postscript (Nachschrift, pp. 204–209) was added containing the results of subsequent observations, and especially remarks on the genus Amia and Carl Vogt's researches thereon. This postscript was, in many respects, a reproduction of an article published in the Monatsberichte.

The memoir next in importance from the great light which was shed upon many obscure questions of Palæichthyology was contributed by England's great naturalist, Prof. Huxley.[3] In the article in question, though professedly upon the Devonian fishes, all that could render intelligible the forms treated was called into requisition, and many unexpected relations were demonstrated or approximated.

The discovery of a representative of the *Ceratodontidæ*, a type previously supposed to have become extinct in the triassic epoch, was the next event of importance; the most sagacious recognition of its affinities, evidence of extended knowledge, by its nomenclator (Dr. Krefft, of Melbourne, Australia), provoked earnest investigation of its structure, and to Dr. Günther (see p. xi), we are indebted for an elaborate description thereof. The light derived from this examination was reflected upon the allied extinct types, and it was clearly shown that the order, once regarded as so isolated, had been rich in representatives in the distant past.

And for various other additions to our knowledge of these forms, we are

[1] Published in the Archiv (pp. 138–141) as an appendix (Nachtrag) to his memoir on the Ganoids.

[2] Published originally in the Archiv für Naturgeschichte (9 Jahrg., b. I, p. 292–330), where it appeared with the title "Beiträge zur Kenntniss der natürlichen Familien der Fische," but considerably modified, and especially by the exclusion of the Dipnoans and Ganoid fishes from the series. See, also, pp. 155, 156 (Gobioidei *vice* Cyclopodi), + 159–160 (Scales) 175–176 (Anacanthini), 182 (degrading Goniodontes), 186 (Aplochiton, Microstoma), 187 (Galaxiæ), 188 (Esoces), 190–191 (Clupeidæ), 192 (+ Heteropygii), 193–194 (Apodes).

[3] Huxley (Thomas Henry). Preliminary Essay upon the Systematic Arrangement of the Fishes of the Devonian Epoch, ... < Memoirs of the Geological Survey of the United Kingdom. Figures and Descriptions Illustrative of British organic remains. Decade x., 1861, pp. 1–40.

Indebted to the labors of Agassiz, Lütken[1] (see p. x), Cope (see p. x), and Lankester.

The Ganoids a Natural Group.

It has been objected that the Ganoids do not constitute a natural group, and that the characters (i. e., chiasma of optic nerves and multivalvular bulbus arteriosus) alleged by Müller to be peculiar to the teleostomous forms combined therein, are problematical, and only *inferentially* supposed to be common to the extinct Ganoids so called, and, finally, such objections couched in too strong language have culminated in the assertion that the characters in question are actually *shared* by other physostome fishes.

No *demonstration*, however, has been presented as yet that any physostome fishes do really have the optic chiasma and multivalvular *bulbus arteriosus*, and the statement to the contrary seems to have been the result of a venial misapprehension of Prof. Kner's statements, or the offspring of impressions left on the memory by his assertions, in forgetfulness of his exact words.

But Prof. Kner,[2] in respect to the anatomical characters referred to, merely objects; (1) they are *problematical*, are not confirmable for the extinct types, and were *probably* not existent in certain forms that have been referred to the Ganoids; (2) the difference in number of the valves of the *bulbus arteriosus* among recent Ganoids is so great as to show the unreliability of the character; (3) a spiral valve is developed in the intestine of several osseous fishes ("genera of the so-called intermediate cineoid groups") as well as in Ganoids; and (4) the chiasma of the optic nerves in no wise furnishes a positive character for the Ganoids.[3]

[1] The extended memoir of Dr. Lütken (Om Ganoidernes Begrændsning og Inddeling) contains a valuable résumé of the history, up to 1867, of the Ganoids, as well as a full bibliography relating to the group, and a critical discussion of the forms referred to it.

[2] Kner (Rudolph). Betrachtungen über die Ganoiden, etc. < op. cit. (supra, p. 00), p. 522.

[3] Noch andere der angeführten Merkmale sind geradezu *problematisch*, da sie nur auf muthmaasslichen Voraussetzungen und Annahmen beruhen, nicht aber als wirklich vorhanden nachzuweisen sind. Zu solchen gehören die von J. Müller für lebende Ganoiden hervorgehobenen anatomischen Merkmale: (1) der muskellose Bulbus mit mehreren Klappenreihen, (2) das Chiasma und (3) die Spiralklappe im Darmcanal.

(1) Für die allermeisten fossilen Fische, die für Ganoiden gelten, ist nicht nachweisbar, dass diese Merkmale vorhanden waren und vielmehr mit Grund zu vermuthen, dass sie sämmtlich solchen nicht zukamen, die in alter Zeit als Prototypen späterer Teleostier auftraten, wie z. B. den triasischen Gattungen *Belonorhynchus, Pholidophorus* u.v.a. Allein ganz abgesehen hiervon, so dürfte doch darauf hinzuweisen sein, in welch ungleichem Grade sich diese Merkmale selbst bei den verschiedenen Gattungen der le-

It will be noticed that all these objections (save in the case of the intestinal spiral valve) are hypothetical and vague. The failure of the intestinal spiral valve, as a diagnostic character, has long been conceded, and in this case only have the forms that *prove* the failure been referred to; in the other cases, where it would be especially desirable to have indicated the actual types falsifying the universality or exclusiveness of the characters, they have not been referred to, and the objections must be met as if they were not known to exist.

(1) The characters in question are, in the sense used, problematical, inasmuch as no examination can be made of the soft parts of extinct forms, but with equal force may it be urged that any characters that have not or cannot be *directly* confirmed are problematical, in the case of all other groups (*e. g.*, Mammals), and it can only be replied that the co-ordination of parts has been so invariably verified that all probabilities are in favor of similar co-ordination in any given case.

(2) There is doubtless considerable difference in the number of valves of the *bulbus arteriosus* among the various Ganoids, and even among the species of a single family (*e. g.*, Lepidosteidæ), but the character of Ganoids lies not in the number, more or less, but in the greater number and relations (in contradistinction to the opposite pair[1] of the Teleosts) in conjunction with the development of a *bulbus arteriosus*. In no other forms of Teleostomes have similar relations and structures been yet demonstrated.

(3) The failure of the spiral intestinal valve has already been conceded, and no great stress has ever been laid on the character.

(4) The chiasma of the optic nerves is common to all the known Ganoids, and has not been found in those forms (*e. g.*, *Arapaima*, *Osteoglossum*, and *Clupeiform* types) agreeing with typical physostome Teleosts in the skeleton, heart, etc., but which at the same time resemble most certain Ganoids (*e. g.*, *Amia*) in form.

bemden Ganoiden verbinden; man braucht sich nur [2] der grossen Differenzen in der Zahl der Aortensticl-Klappen bei *Lepidosteus* und *Amia* zu erinnern, oder [3] des Umstandes, dass eine Spiralklappe im Darmcanale unter den lebenden Fischen nicht blos bei Ganoiden, sondern auch bei Selachiern und mehreren Knochenfischen (Gattungen der sogenannten intermediären Clupeiden-Gruppen) und nicht blos im Dünndarme, sondern auch in andern Abtheilungen des Verdauungsrohres sich verfindet, und dass auch [4] die Chiasmabildung keineswegs einen verlässlichen Unterschied der Ganoiden abgibt.—Kner, op. cit., pp. 622-623.

This paragraph is the only one that squarely meets the question of the applicability of the *fundamental* characters of the Ganoids, as given by *Müller*. It need only be added that the ideas respecting *probability* of pertinence must be a reflection from the deductions resulting from a more or less thorough study of the known elements. The question as to the value of the chiasma is certainly disposed of in a very summary manner, but not in an equally satisfactory one.

[1] "The sunfish (*Orthagoriscus*) has four such valves."—Owen, Anat. Vert., I. 474.

Therefore, in view of the evidence hitherto obtained, the arguments against the validity of title, to natural consociation, of the Ganoids have to meet the positive evidence of the co-ordinations noted; the value of such characteristics and co-ordinations can only be affected or destroyed by the demonstration that in all other respects there is (1) very close agreement of certain of the constituents of the subclass with other forms, and (2) inversely proportionate dissimilarity of those forms from any (not all) other of the Ganoids, and consequently evidence *ubi plurima nitent* against the taxonomic value of the characters employed for distinction.

And it is true that there is a greater superficial resemblance between the Hyoganoids and ordinary physostome Teleosts than between the former and the other orders of Ganoids, but it is equally true that they agree in other respects than in the brain and heart with the more generalized Ga-noids. They all have, for example, (1) the paraglenal elements undivided (not disintegrated into hypercoracoid, hypocoracoid, and mesocoracoid), (2) a humerus (simple, or divided—that is, differentiated into metapterygium and mesopterygium), and (3) those with ossified skeletons agree in the greater number of elements in the lower jaw. Therefore, until these co-ordinates fail, it seems advisable to recognize the Ganoids as constituents of a natural series, and especially on account of the superior taxonomic value of modifications of the brain and heart in other classes of Vertebrates, for the same reason, and to keep prominently before the mind the characters in question, it appears also advisable to designate the series, until further discovery, as a subclass.

But it is quite possible that among some of the generalized Teleosts, at least *traces* of some of the characters now considered to be peculiar to the Ganoids may be discovered. In anticipation of such possibility, the author had at first discarded the subclass, recognizing the group only as one of the "superorders" of the Teleostomes, but reconsideration convinces him of the propriety of classification representing known facts and legitimate inferences rather than too much anticipation.

It is remembered that all characters are liable to fail with increasing knowledge, and the distinctness of groups are but little more than the expressions of our want of knowledge of intermediate forms; it may in truth be said that ability to segregate a class into well-defined groups is in ratio to our ignorance of all the terms.

SEQUENCE OF GANOIDS.

The questions, (1) which are the most generalized of the Ganoids, and (2) what is the most natural succession of forms, are not the simple problems they might appear to be, if only the histological condition of the skeleton should be taken into account. If, on the one hand, in such respects, the Chondrosteans appear to approach the Elasmobranchiates most—on the other hand, in the development of the paraglenal, and the structure of the base of the pectoral fin, they differ less from the Ichthyoid Hyoganoids than do the Crossopterygians and the Dipneans. Nevertheless, they seem on the whole to be the more direct representatives of the lineal succession from the Elasmobranchiates, although doubtless very much modified and different ordinally from the unknown immediate representatives. This has been the view or at least the practice of all Ichthyologists except Prof. Cope.

The eminent naturalist referred to has contended that the Chondrosteans were more nearly related to the typical fishes, and has (1) combined them as well as the Hyoganoids with the Teleosteans in a peculiar subclass (Actinopteri), while (2) the Crossopterygians were differentiated as another, and (3) the Dipneans retained with similar rank.

The chief considerations, apparently, which induced Prof. Cope to isolate the Crossopterygians and combine the Chondrosteans with the forms referred to, were the result of his study of the pectoral members and their insertion, and the inference therefrom that there was an essential similarity therein between the Chondrosteans and Teleosts, and a fundamental dissimilarity between them and the Crossopterygians.

Apart from the development of a single or double ceratohyal, which was evidently regarded as of subordinate importance,[1] the only expressed differences between Cope's subclasses Crossopterygia and Actinopteri are found in the constitution of the pectoral fins, viz :—

CROSSOPTERYGIA: "Limbs having the derivative radii of the primary series on the extremity of the basal pieces, which are in the pectoral fin metapterygium, mesopterygium, and propterygium."

ACTINOPTERI: "Primary radii of fore limb parallel with basilar elements, both entering the articulation with scapular arch. Basilar elements reduced to metapterygium and very rarely mesopterygium. Primary radii of posterior limb generally reduced to one rudiment."

The question arises (1) whether the fundamental differences exist which appear to be expressed by the definitions cited; (2) the correlated one, whether too much importance may not have been attached to superficial relations of parts, and too little to fundamental homological relations, and (3) even if the homological relations are as dissimilar as the definitions would indicate, are they coincident with others, and thus really indicative of such high value.

EXCURSUS ON THE PECTORAL LIMB.

The diagnoses in question seem to be partly (i. e., the articulation or not

---

[1] The Dipnoi have a double ceratohyal.

of the radii direct with the scapular arch) the expressions of matters of fact, and partly the interpretation of homologies.

It is assumed (1) that the external basal element of the limb in Chondrosteans is equivalent to the median element (when differentiated) of the plagiostome Elasmobranchiates, and is, therefore, the mesopterygium, and (2) that the propterygium is not developed.

It is not evident, however, why the external element should not be homologous, in part at least, with the propterygium of the Elasmobranchiates. The latter affords a better basis for identification, and it would seem more justifiable—if it must needs be identified with a *single* element —to refer it to the propterygium rather than to the mesopterygium. The mesopterygium may (1) either be represented, in the Chondrosteans, by an independent element ("*r*" in Gegenbaur's *Untersuchungen*), crowded out of place by the intervention of the rays (as in certain Raie), or (2) it may be entirely suppressed through atrophy, or (3) it may be fused with the propterygium (as in the Heterodontidæ and Scymnidæ).[1] In the first case, the *expressed* differences of the Crossopterygians would be confined to the exclusion of the actinosteal element from direct articulation with the scapular arch. But in the most teleostooid of the Ganoids (*Amia*), we find even that condition approximated, only one (of the seven actinosts) being articulated directly with the arch, the rest being connected with the metapterygium.

But even supposing that the mesopterygium is an element entirely wanting in the Hyoganoids and Chondrosteans, two elements (metapterygium and propterygium) are developed in those forms in common with the Crossopterygians, and which are wanting in the Teleosts. It is not evident why the development of a mesopterygium should be of importance so much superior to that of the other two elements, or why the mere fact that the articulation of the actinosts with the scapular arch should be of such paramount significance as to justify the combination of all forms agreeing therein (including the Chondrosteans and all Teleost fishes), and the separation therefrom, as co-ordinate terms, of forms not agreeing therein.

But it is true that the evidence appears to be somewhat contradictory as to the relations of the forms distinguished by the structure of the pectoral limbs as well as the scapular arch. On the one hand, the Chondrosteans (rather than Crossopterygians) agree with the Hyoganoids in the construction of the paragienal element as well as the pectoral member; on the other hand, the Crossopterygians appear to agree more with the Elasmo-

---

[1] Most naturalists would probably prefer either of these interpretations to the homological representation in Chondrostean, by a mesopterygium disintegrated and represented by apparent rays.

branchiates, and less with the Hyoganoids, in these respects. But the Crossopterygians agree with the latter much better in the composition of the skull and squamation, and the question therefore arises whether it is more probable that the Crossopterygians should have attained that specialised similarity to the Hyoganoids from an independent origin, or whether they should have departed (after having received such characters from a common progenitor) in the structure of the scapular arch and the pectoral member, and whether the *apparent* greater similarity in those respects to the Elasmobranchiates is not rather adaptive, or the result of simplicity of structure of the paraglenal. Possibly, the following hypothesis may approximate the truth, and account for the divergencies of the several types.

The Acanthodeans of the devonian and following epochs may be the nearest of kin known to the representatives of the direct line of descent from the typical Elasmobranchiates; the development of two marginal (external and internal) spines in the pectoral limb may lend significance to the specialized condition of the metapterygium and propterygium in the pectoral limbs of the succeeding forms, as may also the character of the scales for those of the typical "Ganoid" type.

CHONDROGANOIDS.

The Chondrosteans furnish the most satisfactory evidence of closest relationship with the ancestral stock in the histological condition of the skeleton, the generalized and little concentrated brachial and hyoid apparatus, and the structure of the fins. At the same time they are considerably removed from the direct line of descent.[1]

BRACHIOGANOID AND DIPNOAN OFFSHOOTS.

From the ancestral stock, somewhat more specialized than that from which the Chondrosteans originated, but with approximately the same pattern of pectoral limb, forms may have been developed in which the metapterygium and propterygium (converging towards the base in the Chondrosteans—and Acanthodeans?) finally approximated and grew together; the intervening cartilage (mesopterygium) became ejected and projected backwards, bearing the specialized actinosts on a convex periphery.

(1) From such an ancestor a long line may have descended which finally culminated in the specialized Crossopterygians now known.

(2) From an equally ancient stock, and deviating less in histological characters, the Dipnoans may have descended: in such forms, the metapterygium and propterygium, instead of diverging backwards, may have con-

[1] There are some reasons for thinking that the Selachostomi are the most generalized group of Ganoids.

tinued to grow together, ejecting more and more the mesopterygium. which would become, *pari passu*, correspondingly elongated and extended backwards; finally, it would become segmented, and the actinosts and rays having become lateral instead of terminal, the limb of *Ceratodus* would be developed.

(3) And finally, should the lateral elements and rays of the pectoral fin of *Ceratodus* become (1) successively aborted, and finally (2) entirely atrophied, the limbs of (1) *Lepidosiren* and (2) *Protopterus* would be reproduced.

In view of the varying combinations of the basal elements of the limbs in the Elasmobranchiates (e. g., *Scymnidæ*, in which all are consolidated), the suppositions thus hazarded do not appear to be unreasonable or opposed by histological or developmental principles or facts.

The question, how the limbs of the quadruped Batrachians have become specialized from such members, is foreign to the present inquiry.

HYOGANOIDS.

The question now recurs, what are the relations and nearest of kin of the Hyoganoids ?

A more significant hint appears to be furnished by the structure and form of the scales of some of the representatives of the group, than by any other part of the structure.

The similarity, in form as well as in intimate structure, of the scales of t.e Lepidosteids to those of the Polypterids is so close, and the peculiarities and specialized characters of those scales are so many, that the fishes distinguished by such common characters must have inherited them from a common progenitor. Any other supposition would be in opposition to the strongest probabilities. For it must be remembered that the community of character is not a general one like that between ordinary cycloid or ctenoid scales, but a close one of a very specialized and proportionately suggestive nature. This similarity is also coincident with a corresponding—though not so great—similarity of the skull, especially the suspensorial apparatus, etc.

But while the Polypterids have deviated widely in some respects—and, among others, in their limbs and the connections of the air-bladder and intestinal canal—from the primitive stock, the Lepidosteids, deviating equally in other respects, have done so less in respect to their limbs.

In the Lepidosteids and the Amiids are found the nearest representatives, among the Ganoids, of the line of descent in the direction of the typical fishes, as in the Crossopterygians and Dipnoans are found the nearest living forms in the line leading towards the Batrachians and higher Vertebrates.

GENEALOGICAL TREE OF GANOIDS.

The following table is added as a graphic illustration of the views just unfolded :—

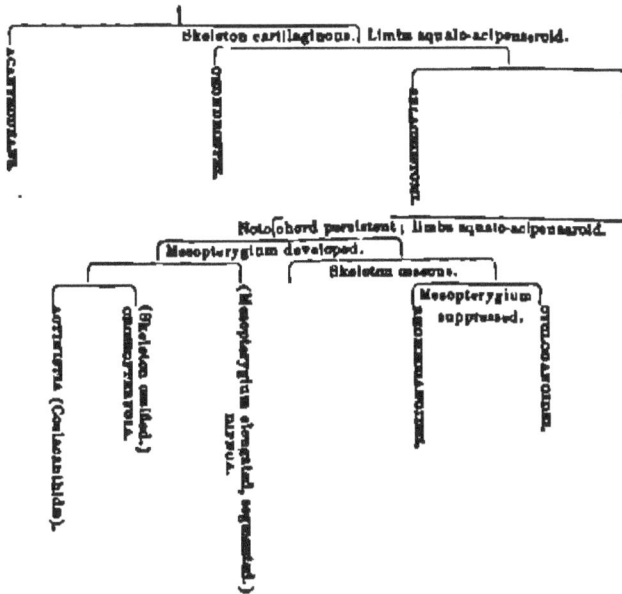

The left branches indicate the more generalized of the contrasted types. The quasi-diagnostic phrases pertain to the succeeding forms, hypothetical or known, till contradicted. The term " squalo-acipenseroid" is intended for a type more generalized than the acipenseroid, and devoid of the special modifications exhibited by the Chondrosteans.

The relations between the various representatives of the Ganoid subclass are very unequal, and they may be advantageously combined into groups more comprehensive than orders. In fine, following out the views just expressed, and subordinating the orders as recommended, we would have the following sequence, starting with the most generalized :—

? ACANTHODEI.

SUPERORDER CHONDROGANOIDEI.

(*Aberrant.*)

Order Chondrostei.

Order Glaniostomi.

SUPERORDER BRACHIOGANOIDEI.

(*Leading to the Dipnoans.*)

Order Actinistia.

Order Crossopterygia.

SUPERORDER DIPNOI.

(*Leading to the Batrachians.*)

Order Sirenoidei.

SUPERORDER HYOGANOIDEI.

(*Leading to the Teleosts.*)

Order Rhomboganoidei.

Order Cycloganoidei.

ON THE TERMS "HIGH" AND "LOW."

The conclusions resulting from the study of the preceding types may render advisable the reconsideration of the reasons of the discrepancy existing among naturalists as to the sequence of the several forms referred to. It has been remarked (p. xx) that the reasons were obvious, and the discrepancies are undoubtedly (1) in part the results of the appreciation of certain truths, and their exaggeration at the expense of others, and to the neglect of the consequences flowing from that cause, and (2) partly of psychological prejudices.

It is a well-assured truth that the Dipnoans are the fishes most nearly related to the Batrachians, and consequently, if nothing else were to be considered, they should undoubtedly be placed next to them. But if this, *per se*, would be a satisfactory procedure, the problem then arises, what shall be done with the other forms? If the Dipnoans are at one extreme and the Leptocardians at the other, between them must necessarily intervene the typical fishes as well as the true Ganoids and the Elasmobranchiates. And if, now, the question of the relative position of the Dipnoans be properly settled, the equally important one—and more vital one on account of the numbers involved—recurs, are we any nearer the truth in approximating next to the Dipnoans, the Elasmobranchiates, the Ganoids, and finally the Teleosts, which last will be next to the *Marsipobranchiates?*

Or, is the question rendered any more easy by first *assuming* that the Elasmobranchiates are "*highest*" and *therefore* (but why?) next to the Batrachians, and then successively arranging the Ganoids, and the Teleosts, still retaining the last *nearest to the Marsipobranchiates?* Admitting that the Dipnoans and (*causa argumenti*) the Elasmobranchiates are the nearest allies of the Batrachians, are the Teleosts the nearest allies of the Marsipobranchiates? Are they in *any* essential respect more like them than are the others? Does the study of their homologies receive any light from the juxtaposition? Is any advantage gained? On the contrary, are not the questions remaining still more involved by reason of such sequence? Is not the natural sequence from the generalized to the specialized unnaturally interrupted and reversed? The answers are not dubious.

Again recalling the universal admission of the "low" or, rather, generalized attributes of the Leptocardians, we have in the ciliated clefts of their pharyngeal sack the first (known) rudiments of a specialized branchial apparatus; an enormous advance is exemplified in the branchial apparatus of the Marsipobranchiates (1. Hyperotreti, 2. Hyperoartii) which nevertheless is (it may be safely said) obviously homologous—*i. e.* homogenetic—with that of the Leptocardians; another advance, less but still very decided, is exhibited in the branchial apparatus of the Elasmobranchiates, while in the Chondrostean and other Ganoids successively, more specialized phases are developed, and all in the *direction of the Teleosts.* We have, in these phases, an apt exemplification of the same concentration towards and in the head as is exhibited by the Tetradecapod and Decapod Crustaceans in their segments and appendages, and which have furnished to the learned Dana the first foundations for his hypothesis of cephalization. And from whatever standpoint we view the series of fishes, the facts of structure, of homologies, and of affinities receive the most light by their exhibition in the sequence advocated, *i. e.*, Leptocardia, Marsipobranchia, Pisces elasmobranchii, Pisces ganoidei, and Pisces teleostei.

And while most naturalists would probably not be indisposed to admit the natural character of the sequence up to the Dipnoans, the desire to have those forms in juxtaposition to the Batrachians and an exclusiveness of attention to that question might result in cutting the gordian knot by effecting that juxtaposition and practically ignoring the other difficulties.[1]

Two questions are principally involved in this consideration.

First. What is the *fish* most nearly to the Batrachians, and consequently to the quadruped vertebrates generally?

---

[1] Probably some of the results in systematic zoology are attained by (1) commencing with Man as the highest, and then (2) approximating successively certain forms, on account of real or supposed affinities, and with little care as to where other forms, whose affinities are less obvious, may lead.

Second. To what other *forms* is that *fish* most nearly related?

(1.) In response to the first question, no doubt has been expressed, the admission that the Dipnoans (and *à fortiori* the Lepidosirenids) are most nearly allied to the Batrachians being universal, even among those who place in the "highest" rank the Elasmobranchiates.

(2.) In response to the second question, the admission (*now* universal) that the Dipnoans are *fishes* determines the question that they are to be *treated* as fishes, and *collocated* in the series of fishes.

And now, if it becomes necessary to enumerate the forms of animals in a linear series, there are the *alternatives* of doing so at the expense of one or the other classes, for (it is scarcely necessary to add) a linear series cannot exhibit all the affinities of living beings.

But it being admitted that the Dipnoans are *Fishes*, it would surely be unreasonable to *overturn* the natural series of the latter *only* to exhibit representatives thereof in juxtaposition to the Batrachians. The alternative then remains to accommodate ourselves to the facts of the case, to build upon the sure foundations furnished by the concurrent admission of what are the most generalized types, and then successively approximating whatever forms are *most nearly related* to the preceding, and without necessary consideration of where we may end—for, commencing aright, we cannot wander very far from the right path.

And if it is admitted that the sequence up to the Dipnoans is not an unnatural one, we have chiefly to inquire what are the forms most nearly related to *them*. It must be admitted that (among living forms) the Crossopterygians are nearest related on one side, and the Batrachians on the other, but the former in very much closer bonds than the latter. And with this concession, we have next to inquire what are the most nearly related to the Crossopterygians. And, in the direction of the Teleosts, it can scarcely be denied that the Hyoganoids are such forms. The relations of the last to the Teleosts are so obvious that it is unnecessary to proceed further.

And if it be demanded, how then can the facts be best expressed? reference may be made to the genealogist. He has to deal with similar problems so far as linear sequence is concerned, and the methods employed by him may be advantageously adapted in biological taxonomy.

Let the Dipnoan be considered as the oldest representative of the ancestral stock equally of the Fishes and of the Batrachians, from which the respective forms have descended, diverging more and more in the course of time. Of course, the Dipnoan will be more nearly related to the Batrachians than the Fishes diverging from the same stem—as the grandparent is more nearly related to the children of two sons than such grandchildren by the different sons are to each other.

But the genealogist takes the oldest branch of the family, and continues to project the series formed by the representatives thereof till it is exhausted, and then recommences with the next.

In like manner, may we take, as the quasi-eldest, the form most like (in essential features) the most generalized type, and continue the series till it is exhausted.

Applying the hint to the problem under consideration, we may take the Crossopterygian as the most nearly related to the Dipnoan, and the representative of the quasi-eldest branch, and continue the series by the successive juxtaposition of the forms next most allied till the pisciform series is exhausted. Then may we resume the broken thread, and recommence from the same ancestral stock with the quasi-younger branch, the Batrachian, and treat it in the same manner. In this way, the natural sequence of types would be preserved, and the least confusion engendered.

And almost all the doubt and obscurity that reign over such questions result from the confusion between the terms high and low with generalized and specialized.

Inasmuch, for example, as the Dipnoan is (1) the most generalized, and therefore (2) more nearly related to the Batrachian than the typical fishes, because (1) of that nearer affinity, and (2) the recognition of the quadruped type as "highest," it is called "higher" than the fishes.

Perhaps there are no words in science that have been productive of more mischief and more retarded the progress of biological taxonomy than those words, pregnant with confusion, High and Low, and it were to be wished that they might be erased from scientific terminology. They deceive the person to whom they are addressed; they insensibly mislead the one who uses them. Psychological prejudices and fancies are so inextricably associated with the words that the use of them is provocative of such ideas. The words generalized and specialized, having become almost limited to the expression of the ideas which the scientific biologist wishes to unfold by the other words, can with great gain be employed in their stead.

TELEOST SERIES.

TELEOCEPHALI

Among the most generalized of the typical fishes, and which have been by common consent regarded as most nearly allied to the Ganoids, are the physostomous Teleocephals, best known under the forms of the *Cyprinids*, *Clupeids*, and *Salmonids*. With these, the Pikes, Scomberesocids, and Perches, and, in fact, all those forms most familiar to men at large, numerous as they are, appear to agree in all material respects as to skeletal peculiarities and the character of the brain. With the reservations already

(p. 00) made and those of like character, it may be said that a *general*
description of the skull and shoulder girdle of a cod, a perch, a mullet, a
pike, a salmon, or an electrical eel would *almost* equally well apply to the
one as to the other, or any other Teleostean fish, so far as the *simple
number* and *essential connections* of the bones are concerned. The frontal
bones may be single or double, the anterior sphenoid (Cuv.) may be present or absent, the palatine and pterygoid bones may be distinct, or (as
in the electrical eel) in part fused together, the scapular arch may be
attached by one or two processes to the skull, a mesocoracoid may or
may not be persistent, and even the paraglenal bones may be quasi-car-
tilaginous, but the agreement in other respects is so close in contrast with
the representatives of other orders, that the exigencies of classification
seem to be best met by the union of all such in one order. In all, the
deviations in the skull are comparatively slight, and the scapular arch
is composed of a post-temporal and posterotemporal, the latter connecting
with the proscapula, while the paraglenal or coracoid is differentiated into at
least a hypercoracoid and a hypocoracoid, the latter two bearing the actl-
osts which are generally four or (rarely) five in number. With the posterotemporal or proscapula is connected a "postclavicle" from which is generally developed a second distal bone, and sometimes (in Clupeidæ) several.
The brain, heart, and vascular system generally, and hyo-branchial apparatus are fundamentally similar, but exhibit (especially the last) minor
modifications that indicate narrower differences, and that may be used in
the distinction of inferior groups. For all the forms possessing the common
characters alluded to, may be retained the ordinal name TELEOCEPHALI,
already referred to.

If a typical physostome fish (e. g., Clupeid) and a specialized physoclyst
form (e. g., *Perca, Blennius*) are contrasted, the differences certainly appear
to be considerable, and are exhibited in (1) the presence or absence of a
ductus pneumaticus, (2) the position of ventrals, abdominal or anterior, (3)
the presence or absence of a mesocoracoid, (4) the junction of the parietals,
or their separation by the intervention of the supraoccipital, (5) the presence of articulated branching rays or their representation by spines, (6)
the low or comparatively high insertion of the pectoral fins, and (7) the
course of the lateral line, whether decurved in the direction of the abdomen
or curved in the direction of the back. But distinct as these forms appear
to be when contrasted, numerous forms intervene in which the characters
successively disappear, or are combined in different ways, and the most esteemed differential characters (presence or absence of the ductus pneumati-

---

¹ I trust that the reservations and explanations which accompany this statement,
and the connection in which it occurs (the discussions of orders), may prevent me
from being misunderstood.

cns) are found in forms on the one hand so closely related (Cyprinodontids vs. Syncntognalhs) and on the other so much differing from the next adjoining forms, that the demands of classification appear to be best met by their union in one order. Of that order, the typical physostome fishes are among the most generalized.

But while the most generalized of the physostome Teleocephals seems to have inherited and retained, in greater measure than any other forms, the primitive characters of the common progenitors of the Teleost fishes, others seem to present claims, but little inferior to theirs, to the rights of primogeniture. It is, too, quite possible that proofs may yet be produced of the superior rights of such claimants; it may be demonstrated that on the whole, such present more features in common with the ancient types than those forms to which the rank is now conceded, and that the specialized characteristics which now exclude them, are not co-ordinated with other equally specialized characters, and have not the significance they now seem to, but so far as present evidence goes, the claims of the physostome Teleocephals appear to be superior to those of any other forms.

But from an almost equally generalized stock, and without evidence of very close relationship with any existing or known forms, the *Scyphophori* and succeeding families seem to have sprung.

SCYPHOPHORI.

The SCYPHOPHORI appear to be sufficiently differentiated from the physostomous Teleocephali by the characters assigned by Cope, as well as other details of the skeleton, and the structure of the brain. On the whole, they appear to be most nearly related among the Teleocephali to the Gymnonoti.

NEMATOGNATHI.

The NEMATOGNATHI depart still further from the ordinary Teleocephalous type in the composition of the skull, and especially the union *inter se* of various elements, as well as in the shoulder girdle, while the peculiar development of the brain confirms the validity of the separation. Their nearest relations appear to be with the Scyphophori. The nearer affinities claimed to exist between them and the Ganoids are not evident, and even the union of the paraglenal elements is probably the result of coalescence rather than of primitive homogeneity, such as prevails among the Ganoids.

APODES.

The APODES are much diversified among themselves, and have been dismembered by Prof. Cope into several orders, but they have the same common form and greatly increased number of vertebræ, want of ventrals, simple structure of the rays of the fins, restricted branchial apertures, and

(e. g. *Synbranchus*, *Anguilla*, *Murœna*), similar brain, so that in default of sufficient opportunity to study the skeleton,[1] the author provisionally, at least, retains them united, but admitting Cope's orders as suborders. Their affinities through the more generalized forms of the order are possibly with the *Gymnonoti*, but the hints furnished by the elongated body and increased number of vertebræ, etc., may be illusive.

OPISTHOMI.

The *Notacanthidæ* and *Mastacembelidæ* have recently been widely separated,[2] and by Cope, an order (Opisthomi) has been established for the last,[3] but, as long ago shown by Johannes Müller, both the forms in question agree in the withdrawal of the shoulder girdle from the skull, and its connection with the vertebral column, and this character seems sufficient, associated as it is with general agreement in other respects between the two families and great dissimilarity from other fishes, to isolate the forms thus marked as a peculiar order;[4] for this order, the name OPISTHOMI, proposed by Cope for one of its members, will be very appropriate, and may be adopted for the enlarged group. It is not obvious what better place can at present be assigned to them than proximity to the Apodes, although it will probably be eventually found to have closer relations with other forms.

HEMIBRANCHII.

The order HEMIBRANCHII, framed by Cope for the group here adopted, seems to be also well worthy of recognition; and, in addition to the characters assigned by its founder, is distinguished (i. e., *Gasterosteidæ*, *Fistulariidæ*) by the structure of the shoulder girdle and the skull, as shown by Parker in the case of the *Gasterosteidæ* (*Shoulder Girdle*, p. 39).[5] The nearest relations, according to Cope, are apparently with the *Atherinidæ*, but such are not obvious, nor are they more so with the *Siphonognathidæ*, with which they have also been in part compared.

LOPHOBRANCHII.

The order LOPHOBRANCHII, according to Prof. Cope, is most nearly related to the Hemibranchii, and such appears to be probable; some members of the order Hemibranchii (*Fistulariidæ*) had, indeed, been long previously

---

[1] I have only been able to study the osseous structure of *Anguilla* and *Murœna*.

[2] See Günther, Cat., v. 3, Syst. Synopsis, pp. viii. x.

[3] No reference is made by Prof. Cope to the Notacanthidæ in any connection.

[4] Of course, *Tetragonurus*, which Müller, who was unacquainted with it, hinted might belong here, has no relation with the group.

[5] Before I was aware of the peculiarities of the shoulder girdle, and only knowing the characters assigned to the order by Cope, I retained it in the order Teleocephali.

placed in juxtaposition to the Lophobranchii (*e. g.* by J. E. Gray, White, and Canestrini), but, no sufficient reason having been given or being apparent, the collocation has been disregarded.

The order (at least after the exclusion of the family of the Pegasidæ) has been almost universally admitted. The Pegasidæ have been eliminated and raised to ordinal rank by A. Duméril, with the name HYPOSTOMIDES; associated with the ordinary fishes by Steenstrup and Günther; and referred to the order Hemibranchii by Cope. Having seen only alcoholic specimens, and no skeleton of this form, the author has not been able to form an opinion.

PLECTOGNATHI

The order of PLECTOGNATHI has been almost as universally admitted as the former, but has been criticized by M. C. Dareste,[1] and stated to be an unnatural association, whose members had diverse relations.

The fishes combined under this name by Cuvier have, however, many characters in common, and are distinguished by the fusion of the several elements of the lower jaw (dentary, angular, and articular) into one; the intermaxillaries and supramaxillaries are more or less closely united; the interoperculum is reduced to a rod-like element, dissevered from connection with the other bones, advanced far forward, and connected by ligament with the lower jaw; the pre-operculum and operculum are articulated with the hyomandibular bone, and the latter, as well as the sub-operculum, are very much reduced in size. The post-temporal unites, more or less intimately, with the skull; the hypo-coracoid is extended downwards. The brain, vascular system, and closed air-bladder do not differ very much from those of the acanthopterygian fishes.

DARESTE (CAMILLE). Thèses soutenues devant la Faculté des Sciences de Paris, par M. Camille Dareste, Licencié ès-sciences naturelles, Docteur en médecine, Professeur d'Histoire naturelle au Collège Stanislas.—Première Thèse. Recherches sur la classification des Poissons de l'ordre des Plectognathes.—Examen de la place que doit occuper dans la classification le Poisson décrit par S. Volta, sous le nom de *Ostorhinus longirostris*.—Paris. Imprimerie de L. Martinet, ... 1850. [4to., 46 pp.]

———— Recherches sur la classification des poissons de l'ordre des Plectognathes. . . . . < Annales des Sciences Naturelles.—Zoologie, 3e Série, t. 14, 1850, p. 105 –133.

———— Sur les affinités naturelles des poissons de la famille des Balistes. Note de M. C. Dareste, présentée par M. Blanchard. < Comptes Rendus hebdomadaires des séances de l'Académie des Sciences, (Paris), v. 74, pp. 1527–1530. (17 Juin, 1872).

———— On the Natural Affinities of the Balistidæ. < Annals and Magazine of Natural History. 4th series, v. 10, pp. 68–70, July, 1872.
A translation of the preceding.

Some of these characters are *diagnostic*, that is, they distinguish the forms from all others; others may be shared with isolated forms of widely separated groups; but the agreement of the "Plectognaths" among themselves in the many common characters justifies their association together, and the characters that are *peculiar* to them sanction their isolation as a group.

Three well-defined groups exhibit the principal modifications under which the fishes possessing these common characters are developed. They are principally distinguished by the development of the scapular arch (the hypercoracoid is atrophied in the Gymnodonts), the degree of union of the jaws and the dentition, and by the squamation. But while the external differences between those forms are doubtless very considerable, they all share the common characters above enumerated and other less salient ones, and in view of this much nearer connection, in contrast with other forms, seem most decidedly deserving of retention together, in contrast with other fishes, whatever rank may be conferred on the group. Their differences sink into comparative insignificance, when compared with their common characters, and seem not entitled to more than subordinal value, while the group of which they are constituents may be most aptly considered an order, as has been done by almost all ichthyologists. The Scleroderms have furnished the chief basis for dissent as to the homogeneous character of the order, and have been deemed more related to ordinary Acanthopterygian types than to the other admitted Plectognaths. And it is quite true that they (and especially the *Triacanthids*) are much more similar to the ordinary fishes than are the typical Plectognaths. This, however, is quite explicable by the supposition that they are the most generalized, and represent the immediate line of descent, while the others are more specialized. That the likeness, however, is superficial and illusive, is evident from the disagreement from the types they must resemble in form, in anatomical characters, and their agreement therein with the other Plectognaths, as already indicated. Prof. Cope has considered the relations of the order (through the *Triacanthids*, on the one hand, and the *Chaetodontidæ* and *Acronuridæ* on the other) to be most intimate with the Teleocephals at the point indicated, and M. Dareste has contended that the *Balistidæ* are especially related to the *Acanthuridæ*. As there seems to be no proof of any nearer relations elsewhere, the hint furnished by the agreements inducing such belief may be followed in the arrangement and sequence of the order as well as of the families constituting it.

PEDICULATI.

The only order adopted remaining for consideration is that of PEDICU-LATI. The natural character of the association of forms combined therein is obvious, and has never been questioned, and the comparatively slight affinity with them of the *Batrachids*, which were formerly combined with them, is now universally conceded. The chief problem with regard to them, therefore, is confined to the question as to the taxonomic value of the characters distinguishing them from other forms. In consideration of the isolation of the group, the saliency of the characters distinguishing them, and the disturbance their intrusion among the Teleocephals would induce, they are distinguished by ordinal rank. Their relations are most intimate with the Batrachoid and Blennioid forms, and doubtless they have descended from the same common progenitors.

GENETIC RELATIONS AND SEQUENCES.

In further explanation respecting the relations of the various forms, it may be remarked that immediate sequence does not by any means necessarily imply immediate affinities. In view of the complex and manifold relations existing, it is generally only possible in a linear arrangement to indicate the nearest relations on *one* side. The most convenient mode of arranging forms in a linear succession appears to be in series,—that is, taking a number of types and arranging them successively, having regard to the forms next most allied, till the series is exhausted; and then recommencing anew with that series whose first member is most nearly allied to one of the preceding:—in other words, following a genealogical system and assimilating it to a scheme, where we would have a given ancestor, and then (1) eldest son, (1a) eldest grandson, (1b) eldest great-grandson, etc.; and after giving all terms of such lineage, we would recommence with the (2) second son and proceed with his descendants in like manner.

The arrangement to really express such relations or quasi-relations would, however, demand a knowledge of fishes which no one now possesses, and consequently no attempt has been made in this article to exhibit them; frequently, indeed, the relations deemed most probable by the author have been violated in deference to general opinion. But without going into details, the following quasi-genealogical tree will convey the views of the author respecting the relations of the major groups, the first table exhibiting the relations of the more generalized orders, and the last of the orders as well as suborders of the Teleost series. In all cases (except the Vertebrates and Molluscoids), the branch to the left—major as well as minor—indicates the supposed most generalized type of the two or more springing or diverging from the same common stem :—

The names printed in largest capitals indicate branches; those in smaller, classes and subclasses; and those in smallest, orders; whilst suborders are printed in lower case.

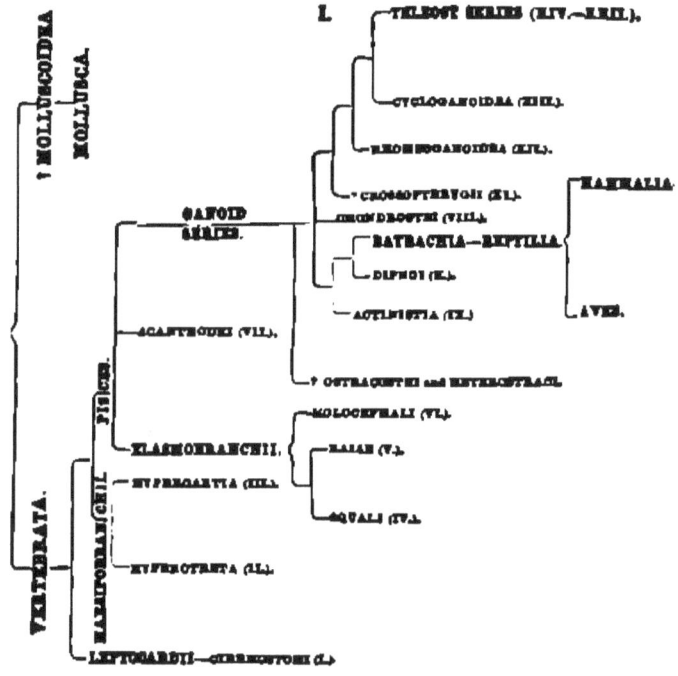

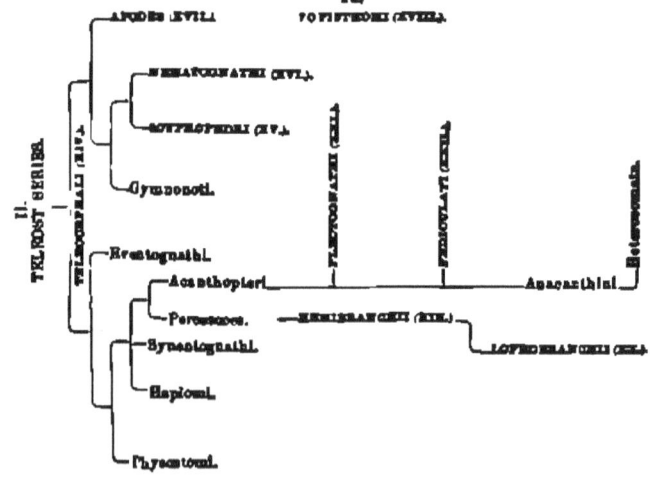

On the assumption that the GYMNONOTI, the SYMBRANCHII, and the NEMATOGNATHI on the one hand, and the APODES on the other, are derivatives from the Physostome Teleocephals or their immediate progenitors, they should, perhaps, be projected after the Teleocephals as successively more differentiated offshoots, but for the present, at least, it is deemed advisable to retain them in the customary position; it is to be understood, however, that they form a diverging line from the supposed common stock, and hence the sequence adopted in the list of families.

In addition to the orders here mentioned, several others appear to be represented by extinct fishes, but we are not sufficiently acquainted with the details of their structure to introduce them with certainty in the system. It may be suggested, however, that one of the orders is constituted of the PLACOGANOIDEI (when restricted to such forms as *Pterichthyidæ* and *Coccosteidæ*); another is represented by the triassic and cretaceous Ganoids with a persistent notochord, ordinary pisciform proportions, and non-lobate pectoral fins, such as the *Caturidæ*. Further details respecting at least the scapular arch and pectoral limb (probably erroneously restored, for the latter, by authors) are requisite before their exact relations can be understood.

FAMILIES.

The families have been much multiplied, and, it may be urged, unduly so, and such may really be the case, but as analysis should precede synthesis, and as many of the more comprehensive families have either not received diagnoses common to and at the same time peculiar to all their constituents; or, in case of applicable diagnoses, the characters are of suspicious value, it has been deemed best to isolate the groups as families, and allow them to stand on their own merits. Several of the families admitted (e.g., *Gadiform*, *Labyrinthiciform*, *Scombriform*, *Perciform*, *Siluriform*), are, however, of very dubious value, and are only provisionally adopted and kept in prominence to attract future examination.

There will doubtless always exist more or less difference of opinion as to the taxonomic values of groups, and all that can be hoped for is essential concurrence of views as to the mutual relations of the various groups and their respective degrees of subordination. Ichthyology has not yet, however, reached that stage wherein even an approximate concurrence in any of these points is possible; and it is not to be wondered at that the greatest difference of opinion should prevail with respect to families. Much of this dissent is due to the fact that certain groups stand isolated from others, and the relations *inter se* of the constituents of such groups are so obvious and evidently suggestive, and contrast so strongly with any other group that, although many and very marked dif-

ferences exist among the constituents, they are overshadowed by the
closer agreement as compared with other groups, and the tendency,
therefore, is to depreciate their value. The NEMATOGNATHI is a case in
point. The ordinal or even subordinal value of the group has been
admitted by few, and generally it is considered as a member of the "order
Physostomi," and as it is really a natural and homogeneous group and
strongly contrasts with any other, by many it has been endowed with only
family rank. Yet the internal and external differences existing within
its limits are very great, and really as obvious and by every analogy as
important as those which the mind has become habituated to consider as
of family value in other cases. And furthermore, the anatomical characters differentiating the group from others are many, striking, and, as shown
by the extent of variation within other groups, very important. The
exigencies of classification, therefore, seem to demand in such a case
ordinal distinction, and then the constituents of the group naturally resolve
themselves into sections whose importance, not being weighed in bulk
against another family, can be appreciated, and the mind is prepared to
admit their superior value.

ACKNOWLEDGMENTS, ETC.

Among those recent works mentioned in the bibliography or incidentally
in the introduction, he has been especially benefited by the memoir of
Prof. Cope, so often referred to. If he has sometimes found reason to
express dissent from that eminent naturalist, it is because the importance
of the memoir in question and the extensive knowledge of its author, have
induced him to review and weigh the evidence affecting the questions in
dispute. And the superior ability and learning of Prof. Cope appeared
to demand reasons for any dissent from his views.

In order to enhance the usefulness of the catalogue, references are made
to Dr. Günther's "Catalogue of Fishes in the British Museum," that being
emphatically the *vade-mecum* for the working ichthyologist, and necessary
to be constantly referred to for identifications, verifications, or references.
In addition, in some cases, references are made to other publications, and
when the names repeated from such authorities are not recognized by or
are different from those employed by Dr. Günther, or when they accompany
different groups, the reference to Günther's work is generally abbreviated
and inclosed in parentheses after the primary reference, thus, "(G. lil., 200
–205)."

Specific acknowledgment is due to the greatest of Spanish naturalists,
Prof. Poey, of Havannah, Cuba, for his courteous attentions for many
years, especially manifested in the transmission, for my use, of the fishes of
Cuba, including many of the types of his new species; I am also indebted

to him for the skulls and more or less of the skeletons of numerous species, and among them of such forms as *Polymixia*, *Scombrops*, *Etelis*, *Platyinius*, *Brotula*, *Lucifuga*, and the rarer forms of other families. I have likewise, through the courtesy of the officers in charge, been able to make free use of the Army Medical Museum.

Acknowledgments are also due to Mr. J. CARSON BREVOORT, of Brooklyn, and to Prof. O. C. MARSH, and Mr. OSCAR HAROER, of Yale College, for the loan of books, and other bibliographical facilities.

In conclusion, the author begs to renew the assertion that the list is in the strictest sense a temporary one, and merely preliminary to renewed investigations, and that the sequence of families is not to be regarded as the expression of the views of the author, except in part. The true exposition of his present views respecting the system are embodied in the preceding essay, and especially in the discussion of the sequence of forms.

Comparative diagnoses, embodying the chief anatomical characteristics of the orders and suborders in analytical tables, had been prepared for an appendix to this volume, but it has been finally deemed by the author best to defer the publication to a future time, and until he has been able to examine the anatomy of several doubtful forms. Immediate insertion is the less called for inasmuch as the remarks in the course of this Introduction will suffice to give an idea of the characters of most of the larger groups adopted.

FAMILIES OF FISHES.

Class PISCES.
Series TELEOSTOML
Sub-Class TELEOSTEI.
PLECTOGNATHI.
Gymnodontes.

1. Orthagoriscidae   Gymnodontes (Molina), Gthr. viii, 269, 317.
2. Tetrodontidae   Gymnodontes (Tetrodontina), Gthr. viii, 269, 270.
3. Triodontidae   Gymnodontes (Triodontina), Gthr. viii, 269, 270.

Ostracodermi.

4. Ostraciontidae   Sclerodermi (Ostraciontina) Gthr. viii, 207, 255.

Sclerodermi.

5. Balistidae   Sclerodermi (Balistina), Gthr. viii, 207, 211.
6. Triacanthidae   Sclerodermi (Triacanthina), Gthr. viii, 207, 208.

LOPHOBRANCHII.

Syngnathi.

7. Hippocampidae   Syngnathidae (Hippocampi-
na), Gthr. viii, 153, 194.
8. Syngnathidae   Syngnathidae (Syngnathina).
Gthr. viii, 153, 154.

Solenostomi.

9. Solenostomidae   Solenostomidae, Gthr. viii,
150.

PEDICULATI.

10. Malthcidae   Malthaeidae,Gill,P.A.N.S.Ph.,
1863,89. (G.iii,200–205.)
11. Lophiidae   Lophiidae, Gill, P. A. N. S. Ph.,
1863,89. (G. iii,178–182.)
12. Ceratiidae   Ceratiidae, Gill, P.A.N.S. Ph.,
1863, 89. (G. iii, 205.)
13. Antennariidae   Antennariidae, Gill, P. A. N. S.
Ph.,'63,89. (G.iii,182–200.)

TELEOCEPHALI.

Heterosomata.

14. Soleidae   Pleuronectidae, Gthr. iv, 399,
462–504.
15. Pleuronectidae   Pleuronectidae, Gthr. iv, 399,
401–457.

8

16. Macruridae	Macruridae, Gthr iv, 390–398.
17. Congrogadidae	Ophidiidae (Congrogadina), Gthr. iv, 370, 388–389.
18. Fierasferidae	Ophidiidae (Fierasferina), Gthr. iv, 370, 381–384.
19. Ophidiidae	Ophidiidae (Ophidiina), Gthr. iv, 370, 376–380.
20. Brotulidae	Ophidiidae (Brotulina), Gthr iv, 370, 371–376. •
21. Brotulophididae	Ophidiidae (Brotulina), Gthr. iv, 370, 375.
22. Bregmacerotidae	Gadidae, Gthr. iv, 326, 368–369.
23. Raniccpitidae	Gadidae, Gthr. iv, 326, 367–368.
24. Gadidae	Gadidae, Gthr. iv, 326, 327–364.
25. Merluciidae	Gadidae, Gthr. iv, 326, 344–346.
26. Lycodidae	Lycodidae, Gill, P. A. N. S. Phil., iv, 319–326.

ANACANTHINI? INCERTAE SEDIS.

| 27. Ateleopodidae | Ateleopodidae, Gthr. iv, 318, 398. |

4

28. Xenocephalidae,	Anacanthini gadoidei (Appendix), Gthr. iv, 399.
29. Ammodytidae	Ophidiidae (Ammodytina), Gthr. iv, 384, 387.
30. Gadopsidae	Gadopsidae, Gthr. iv, 318. (D. x–xi, 25–26. A. iii, 18–19.)

ACANTHOPTERI.

(Blennoidea.)

31. Cryptacanthidae	Cryptacanthidae, Gill, Can. Nat.,1865. (G. iii, 206, 291.)
32. Stichaeidae	Stichaeidae, Gill, P. A. N. S. Phil. (Gthr. iii, 206, 280.)
33. Xiphidiontidae	Xiphidiontidae, Gill, Can. Nat., 1865. (G. iii, 206, 285–291.)
34. Acanthoclinidae	Acanthoclinidae, Gthr. iii, 297–298.
35. Chaenopsidae	Chaenopsidae, Gill, An. Lyc. N. H. N. Y., viii, 141–144.
36. Nemophididae	Nemophididae, Gill, An. Lyc. N. H. N. Y., viii, 138–141.
37. Anarrhicadidae	Anarrhicadidae, Gill, Can. Nat.,1865. (G. iii, 208–211.)
38. Cebidichthyidae	Cebidichthyidae, Gill, P. A. N. S. Phil., 1865. (G. iii, 206.)
39. Blenniidae	Blenniidae, Gthr. iii, 206, 211–279.

40. Pataecidae   Blenniidae, Gthr. iii, 206, 292–293.

(*Batrachoidea.*)

41. Batrachidae   Batrachidae, Gthr. iii, 166–177.

(*Trachinoidea.*)

42. Leptoscopidae   Leptoscopoidae, Gill, P. A. N. S. Phil., 1862, 501–505.
43. Dactyloscopidae   Leptoscopoidae, Gill, P. A. N. S. Phil., 1862, 501, 505–506.
44. Uranoscopidae   Uranoscopoidae, Gill, P. A. N. S. Phil., 1861, 108–117.
45. Trachinidae   Trachinidae, Gthr. ii, 225, 232–237.

(*Trichodontoidea.*)

46. Trichodontidae   Trichodontoidae, Gill, P. A. N. S. Ph., 1861, 514. (G. ii, 250.)

(*Gobiesocoidea.*)

47. Gobiesocidae   Gobiesocidae, Gthr. iii, 489–515.
48. Liparididae   Cyclopteridae (Liparidina), Gthr. iii, 154, 154–158.
49. Cyclopteridae   Cyclopteridae (Cyclopterina), Gthr. iii, 154, 158–165. .

(*Gobioidea.*)

(*Cottoidea.*)

(*Pharyngognathi.*)

61. Siphonognathidae   Labridae (Scarina), Gthr. iv, 65, 243–244.

62. Labridae   Labridae, Gthr. iv, 65, 69–208, 240–243.

63. Pomacentridae   Pomacentridae,   Gthr.   iv, 2–64.

64. Cichlidae   Chromides, Gthr. iv, 265–316.

65. Embiotocidae   Embiotocidae, Gthr. iv, 244–251.

66. Gerridae   Gerridae, Gthr. iv, 252–264; (also, i, 339–354.)

(Labyrinthici.)

67. Helostomidae   Helostom[idae], Cope, Tr. Phil. Soc. xiv, 459.   (G. iii, 377.)

68. Anabantidae   Anabantidae, Cope, Tr. Phil. Soc. xiv, 459. (Gthr. iii, 372.)

69. Osphromenidae   Osphromenidae. Cope, Tr. Phil. Soc. xiv, 459. (Gthr. iii, 382.)

(Polynematoidea.)

70. Polynemidae   Polynemidae, Gthr. ii, 319–333.

(Acronuridae.)

71. Acanthuridae   Acronuridae, Gthr. iii, 325–356.

72. Amphacanthidae   Teuthididae, Gthr. iii, 313–324.

(Chaetodontoidea.)

73. Toxotidae   Squamipennes (Toxotina), Gthr. ii, 66–68.

74. Chaetodontidae   Squamipennes (Chaetodontina), Gthr. ii, 1, 3–57.

75. Ephippiidae   Squamipennes (Chaetodontina), Gthr. ii, 1, 57–62.

(Scombroidea.)   .

76. Xiphiidae   Xiphiidae. Gthr. ii, 511–512.

77. Trichiuridae   Lepturoidae, Gill, P.A.N.S.Ph., 1863, 224. (G. ii, 342–349.)

78. Scombridae   Scombridae, Gill, P.A.N.S.Ph., 1862, 124. (G. ii, 349–373.)

79. Carangidae   Carangidae, Gill, P.A.N.S.Ph., 1862, 430. (G. ii, 419–485.)

80. Drepanidae   Squamipennes (Drepane), Gthr. ii, 1, 62.

81. Coryphaenidae   Scombridae (Coryphaenina pt), Gthr. ii, 404.

82. Nematistiidae   Nematistiidae, Gill, P. A. N. S. Phil., 1862, 258.

83. Stromateidae   Scombridae (Stromateina), Gthr. ii, 397–404.

84. Zenidae   Zenidae, Gill, P. A. N. S. Phil., 1862, 126. (G. ii, 393–396.)

85. Pteraclididae   Scombridae (Coryphaenina), Gthr. ii, 410.

86. Bramidae   Scombridae (Coryphaenina), Gthr. ii, 408.

87. Lamprididae   Scombridae (Coryphaenina), Gthr. ii, 415.

88. Dianidae   Scombridae (Coryphaenina), Gthr. ii, 413.

89. Kurtidae   Carangidae (Kurtina), Gthr. ii, 508–510.

90. Capridae   Carangidae (Carangina), Gthr. ii, 495.

91. Nomeidae   Scombridae (Nomeina), Gthr. ii, 387.

(Sillaginoidea.)

92. Sillaginidae   Sillaginoidae, Gill, P. A. N. S. Phil., 1861, 501–507.

93. Chaenichthyidae   Chaenichthyoidae, Gill, P. A. N. S. Phil., 1861, 507–510.

94. Harpagiferidae   Harpagiferoidae, Gill, P. A. N. S. Phil., 1861, 510–512.

95. Nototheniidae   Notothenioidae, Gill, P. A. N. S. Phil., 1861, 512–522.

96. Bovichthyidae   Bovichthyoidae, Gill, P. A. N. S.Ph.,1861,514. (G.ii,225.)

97. Latilidae   Latiloidae, Gill, P. A. N. S. Ph., 1861, 514. (G. ii, 359–361.)

(Mulloidea.)

98. Mullidae   Mullidae   Gthr.   i,   397–
411.

(Polymixoidea.)

99. Polymixiidae   Berycidae (Polymixia), Gthr.
i, 8 (16–19).

(Berycoidea.)

100. Monocentridae   Berycidae, Gthr. i, 8 (8–
12).

101. Berycidae   Berycidae, Gthr. i, 8 (12–
50).

(Sciaenoidea.)

102. Sciaenidae   Sciaenidae, Gthr. ii, 265–
318.

(Percoidea.)

103. Sparidae   Sparidae (Cantharina, Sargina,
Pagrina), Gthr. i, 412.

104. Pimelepteridae   Sparidae   (Pimelepterina),
Gthr. i, 497.

105. Maenididae   Pristipomatidae, Gthr. i, 272.
(In part.)

106. Pristipomatidae   Pristipomatidae, Gthr. i, 272.
(In part.)

107. Centrarchidae   Centrarchoidae, Gill, Am. J. S.
& A., (2s), xxxvii, 92.

108. Serranidae   Percidae (Serranina), Gthr. i, 51, 81.

109. Percidae   Percidae (Percina), Gthr. i, 51, 58.

110. Centropomidae   Percidae (Centropomus), Gthr. i, 51, 79. '

(*Physoclysti incertae sedis.*)

(*Pegasoidea.*)

111. Pegasidae   Pegasidae, Gthr. viii, 146–149.

(*Priacanthoidea.*)

112. Priacanthidae   Percidae (Priacanthina), Gthr. i, 215.

(*Hoplegnathoidea.*)

113. Hoplegnathidae   Hoplegnathidae, Gthr. iii, 357–358.

(*Nandidae* Gthr.)

114. Nandidae   Nandidae (Nandina), Gthr. iii, 362, 367–369.

115. Plesiopidae   Nandidae (Plesiopina), Gthr. iii, 362, 363–366.

(*Polycentridae.*)

116. Polycentridae   Polycentridae, Gthr. iii, 370–371.

(*Cirrhitidae.*)

117. Cirrhitidae   Cirrhitidae, Gill, P. A. N. S. Phil., 1862, 102–124.

(*Acanthopterygii*, § ii, Gthr.)

118. Aphredoderidae   Aphredoderidae,   Gthr.   i,
271.

(*Sphyraenoidea.*)

119. Sphyraenidae   Sphyraenidae, Gthr. ii, 334-
341.

(*Echeneidoidea.*)

120. Echeneididae   Scombridae (Echeneis), Gthr.
ii, 354, 376-385.

(*Oxudercidae.*)

121. Oxudercidae   Oxudercidae,   Gthr.   iii,
165.

(*Comephoridae.*)

122. Comephoridae   Comephoridae,   Gthr.   iii,
299.

(*Acanthopterygyii*, § iv, Gthr.)

123. Trachypteridae   Trachypteridae, Gthr. iii, 300-
311.

(*Acanthopterygii*, § iii, Gthr.)

124. Lophotidae   Lophotidae, Gthr. iii, 312.

(*Luciocephalidae.*)

125. Luciocephalidae   Luciocephalidae,   Gthr.   iii,
390.

(Acanthopterygii channiformes, Gthr.)

126. Ophiocephalidae   Ophiocephalidae, Gthr. iii, 468–483.

(Acanthopterygii blenniformes, § ii, Gthr.)

127. Trichonotidae   Trichonotidae, Gthr. iii, 484–485.

(Acanthopterygii blenniformes, § i, Gthr.)

128. Cepolidae   Cepolidae, Gthr. iii, 486–489.

(Acanthopterygii gobiesociformes, § ii, Gthr.)

129. Psychrolutidae   Psychrolutidae, Gthr. iii, 516–517.

PERCESOCES.

(Cope, Tr. Am. Phil. Soc., xiv, 456, 457.)

130. Atherinidae   Atherinidae   (Atherinina), Gthr. iii, 391, 392–406.

131. Tetragonuridae   Atherinidae (Tetragonurina), Gthr. iii, 391, 407.

132. Mugilidae   Mugilidae, Gthr. iii, 409–467.

HEMIBRANCHI.

(Cope, Tr. Am. Phil. Soc., xiv, 456, 457.)

(H. Gasterosteiformes.)

(Gasterosteoidea.)

133. Gasterosteidae   Gasterosteidae,   Gthr.   i, 1–7.

134. Aulorhynchidae   Aulorhynchoidae, Gill, P. A. N. S., Phil., 1862, 233.

(*Aulostomoidea.*)

135. Aulostomidae   Fistulariidae, Gthr. iii, 529, 535–538.

136. Fistulariidae   Fistulariidae, Gthr. iii, 529–534.

(*H. Centrisciformes.*)

137. Centriscidae   Centriscidae Gthr. iii, 518–524.

138. Amphisilidae   Centriscidae, Gthr. iii, 518, 524–527.

SYNENTOGNATHI.

139. Belonidae   Scomberesocidae, Gthr. vi, 233, 234–256.

140. Scomberesocidae   Scomberesocidae, Gthr. vi, 233, 256–298.

HAPLOMI.

(Cope, Tr. Am. Phil. Soc., xiv, 452, 455.)

(*Amblyopoidea.*)

141. Amblyopidae   Heteropygii, Gthr. vii, 1–2; Putn., Am. Nat., vi, 6–30.

(*Cyprinodontoidea.*)

154. Stomiatidae   Stomiatidae, Gthr. v, 424–428.

155. Scopelidae   Scopelidae (Saurina), Gthr. v, 393, 404–417.

156. Aulopidae   Aulopidae, Cope, Tr. Am. Phil. Soc.,xiv,455. (G.v,303,402.)

157. Synodontidae   Scopelidae (Saurina), Gthr. v, 393, 394–404.

158. Microstomidae   Coregonidae, Cope,Tr. Am. Ph. Soc., xiv, 455. (G. vi, 1.)

159. Salmonidae   Salmonidae, Cope, Tr. Am. Ph. Soc., xiv, 455. (G. vi, 1.)

160. Salangidae   Salmonidae (Salangina), G. vi, 1, 205.

(*Paralepidoidea.*)

161. Alepidosauridae   Scopelidae (Alepidosaurina), Gthr. v, 393, 420–423.

162. Paralepididae   Scopelidae (Paralepidina), Gthr. v, 393, 418–420.

(*Alepocephalidae.*)

163. Alepocephalidae   Alepocephalidae, Gthr. vii, 477.

(*Gonorhynchidae.*)

164. Gonorhynchidae   Gonorhynchidae, Gthr. vii, 373.

17

176. Cobitidae   Cyprinidac (Cobitina), Gthr.
    vii, 3, 344.
177. Homalopteridae   Cyprinidae (Homalopterina),
    Gthr. vii, 3, 340–343.
178. Kneriidae   Kneriidae, Gthr. vii, 371–
    372.

GYMNONOTI.

(*Glanencheli*, Cope, Tr. Am. Phil. Soc., xiv, 455.)

179. Sternopygidae   Sternopygidae, Cope, Tr. Am.
    Ph. Soc., xiv, 455. (G. viii, 1.)
180. Electrophoridae   Gymnotidae, Cope, Tr. Am.
    Ph. Soc., xiv, 455. (G. viii, 1.)

SCYPHOPHORI.

(Cope, Tr. Am. Phil. Soc., xiv, 455.)

181. Mormyridae   Mormyridae, Gthr. vi, 214–
    224.
182. Gymnarchidae   Gymnarchidae, Gthr. vi,
    225.

NEMATOGNATHI.

(*Hypophthalmidae*, Cope.)

183. Hypophthalmidae   Hypophthalmidae, Cope, op.
    cit. xiv, 454. (G. v, 66–68.)

(*Siluridae*, Cope.)

184. Trichomycteridae   Siluridae (Opisthopterae), G.
    v, 1, 272–277.

185. Siluridae   Siluridae (—), Gthr. v, 1, 30–63, 69–220.

186. Chacidae   Siluridae (Chacina), Gthr. v, 1, 29.

187. Plotosidae   Siluridae (Plotosina), Gthr. v, 1, 23–27.

188. Clariidae   Siluridae (Clarina), Gthr. v, 1, 13–23.

189. Callichthyidae   Siluridae (Hypostomatina), Gthr. v, 1, 225–230.

190. Argiidae   Siluridae (> Hypostomatina), Gthr. v, 1, 222–225.

191. Loricariidae   Siluridae (> Hypostomatina), Gthr. v, 1, 230–265.

192. Sisoridae   Siluridae (Hypostomatina), Gthr. v, 262–265.

(*Aspredinidae*, Cope.)

193. Aspredinidae   Siluridae (Aspredinina), Gthr. v, 3, 266–270.

APODES.

ICHTHYOCEPHALI.

(Cope, Tr. Am. Phil. Soc., xiv, 455.)

194. Monopteridae   Symbranchidae (Symbranchina), Gthr. viii, 12, 14.

Holostomi.

(Cope, Tr. Am. Phil. Soc., xiv, 455.)

195. Symbrachidae   Symbranchidae (Symbranchi-
                    na), Gthr. viii, 12, 14.
196. Amphipnoidae   Symbranchidae (Amphipno-
                    ina), Gthr. viii, 12, 13.

Enchelycephali.

(Cope, Tr. Am. Phil. Soc., xiv, 455.)

197. Muraenesocidae   Muraenidae (Muraenesocina),
                    Gthr. viii, 19, 45.
198. Congridae   Muraenidae   (Anguillina),
                    Gthr. viii, 19, 23.
199. Anguillidae   Muraenidae   (Anguillina),
                    Gthr. viii, 19, 23.

Colocephali.

(Cope, Tr. Am. Phil. Soc., xiv, 416.)

200. Rataburidae   Muraenidae (Ptyobranchina),
                    Gthr. viii, 19, 90.
201. Muraenidae   Muraenidae (——), Gthr. viii,
                    19.

Apodes? incerti sedis.

202. Chilobranchidae   Symbranchidae (Chilobran-
                    china), Gtbr. viii, 12, 17.
203. Nemichthyidae   Muraenidae (Nemichthyina),
                    Gtbr. viii, 19, 21.

204. Synaphobranch- Muraenidae (Synaphobranch-
    idae   ina), Gthr. viii, 19, 22.
205. Saccopharyngidae Muraenidae (Saccopharyng-
              ina), Gthr. viii, 19, 22.

OPISTHOMI.

(Cope, Tr. Am. Phil. Soc., xvi, 456.)

206. Mastacembelidae Mastacembelidae, Gthr. iii,
              539–543.
207. Notacanthidae   Notacanthidae, Gthr. iii, 544–
              545.

Sub-Class GANOIDEI

Super-Order HYOGANOIDEI.

CYCLOGANOIDEI.

208. Amiidae   Amiidae, Gthr. viii, 324–
              325.

RHOMBOGANOIDEI.

209. Lepidosteidae   Lepidosteidae, Gthr. viii, 328–
              331.

Super-Order BRACHIOGANOIDEI.

CROSSOPTERYGIA.

210. Polypteridae   Polypteridae, Gthr. viii, 326–
              328.

Super-Order DIPNOI.

SIRENOIDEI.

Super-Order CHONDROGANOIDEI.

SELACHOSTOMI.

CHONDROSTEI.

Sub-Class ELASMOBRANCHII.

Super-Order HOLOCEPHALI.

HOLOCEPHALI.

Super-Order PLAGIOSTOMI.

RAIAE.

MASTICURA.

217. Cephalopteridae   Myliobatidae (Ceratopterina),
     Gthr. viii, 488, 496–498.

218. Trygonidae   Trygonidae, Gthr. viii, 471–
     488.

PACHYURA.

219. Torpedinidae   Torpedinidae, Gthr. viii, 448–
     455.

220. Raiidae   Raiidae, Gthr. viii, 455–
     471.

221. Rhinobatidae   Rhinobatidae, Gthr. viii, 440,
     441–448.

222. Rhamphobatidae   Rhinobatidae, Gthr. viii, 440,
     440–441.

223. Pristidae   Pristidae, Gthr. viii, 436–
     439.

SQUALL.

RHINAE.

224. Squatinidae   Rhinidae, Gthr. viii, 430–
     431.

GALEI.

225. Heterodontidae   Cestraciontidae, Gthr. viii,
     415–416.

226. Notidanidae   Notidanidae, Gthr. viii, 397–
     399.

227. Rhinodontidae   Rhinodontidae, Gthr. viii, 396.

228. Cetorhinidae   Lamnidae (Selachina), Gthr. viii, 389, 394.

229. Lamnidae   Lamnidae (Lamnina), Gthr. viii, 389, 389–392.

230. Odontaspididae   Lamnidae (Lamnina), Gthr. viii, 389, 392–393.

231. Alopeciidae   Lamnidae (Lamnina), Gthr. viii, 389, 393–394.

232. Sphyrnidae   Carchariidae (Zygaenina), Gthr. viii, 357, 380–383.

233. Galeorhinidae   Carchariidae (Carchariina, Mustelina), G. viii, 357–388.

234. Scylliidae   Scylliidae, Gthr. vi, 400–413.

235. Ginglymostomatidae   Scylliidae, Gthr. vi, 400, 407–409.

236. Crossorhinidae   Scylliidae, Gthr. vi, 400, 413–414.

237. Spinacidae   Spinacidae, Gthr. vi, 417, 418–425.

238. Scymnidae   Spinacidae, Gthr. vi, 417, 425–429.

239. Oxynotidae   Spinacidae, Gthr. vi, 417, 417.

240. Pristiophoridae   Pristiophoridae, Gthr. vi, 431–433.

Class MARSIPOBRANCHII.

HYPEROARTIA.

241. Petromyzontidae   Petromyzontidae, Gthr. viii, 499–509.

HYPEROTRETI.

242. Myxinidae   Myxinidae, Gthr. viii, 510, 510–511.

243. Bdellostomidae   Myxinidae, Gthr. viii, 510, 511–512.

Class LEPTOCARDII.

CIRROSTOMI.

244. Branchiostomidae   Cirrostomi, Gthr. viii, 513–514.

BIBLIOGRAPHY.

Subjoined is a synopsis of the great standard works of descriptive ichthyology, which will give information as to the extent, price, etc., of the works in question, and also some idea respecting the classifications adopted by their authors. The information may be considered as a response to inquiries often made respecting such subjects.

The work of Cuvier and Valenciennes was never completed, and, as will be perceived from the enumeration of contents, included only the Acanthopterygian and Pharyngognathi Teleostei, and incidentally the Anbloids whose relations were not recognised by Valenciennes. Cuvier only contributed the introduction and monographs of families in the first ten volumes, his death having taken place in the year 1832. Valenciennes only is responsible for the rest of the work.

The work of Duméril may be considered as a complement to that of Cuvier and Valenciennes. The death of the author has arrested the further progress of the work.

The work of Dr. Günther is the only complete repertory of the species of fishes published, and, from its cheapness, the most available; it is also subsequent to both the preceding, and therefore in a certain degree supersedes them. No general index has been published yet, but one is promised in connection with an appendix bringing the subject up to date, if circumstances permit.

In order, further, to give some idea of the progress of ichthyology, the titles are given of all the compilations professing to describe the species of fishes known at the periods of their respective publication. These compilations are valuable, however, only to the historian of ichthyology, and are worse than useless to any except an expert in the science.

1738.

ARTEDI (Peter). Petri Artedi Sueci, Medici, Ichthyologia sive opera omnia de Piscibus scilicet: Bibliotheca Ichthyologica. Philosophia Ichthyologica. Genera Piscium. Synonymia Piscium. Descriptiones Specierum—Omnia in hoc opere perfectiora, quam antea alia. Posthuma Vindicavit, Recognovit, Coaptavit et Edidit Carolus Linnaeus, Med. Doct. & Ac. Imper. N. C.—Lugduni Batavorum, Apud Conradum Wishoff. 1738. [8vo., five parts, viz:—

[v. 1.] Petri Artedi Angermannia-Sueci Bibliotheca Ichthyologica seu Historia Litteraria Ichthyologiae in qua Recensio fit Auctorum, qui de Piscibus scripsere, librorum titulis, loco & editionis tempore, additis judiciis, quid quivis Auctor praestiterit, quali method et successu scripserit, disposita secundum saecula in quibus quisquis auctor floruit. Ichthyologia Pars I. — Lugdunum Batavorum, Apud Conradum Wishoff. 1738. [iv, 66, 2 pp.]

[v. 2.] Petri Artedi Sueci Philosophia Ichthyologica in qua quidquid fundamenta Artis absolvit: Characterum scilicet *Genericorum*, *Differentiarum specificarum*, *Varietatum et Nominum Theoria* rationibus demonstratur, et exemplis comprabatur. Ichthyologiae Pars II.—Lugduni Batavorum, Apud Conradum Wishoff. 1738. [iv, 92 pp.]

[v. 3.] Petri Artedi Sueci Genera Piscium. In quibus Systema totum Ichthyologiae proponitur cum Classibus, Ordinibus, Generum Characteribus, Specierum Differentiis, Observationibus plurimis. Redactis Speciebus 242 ad Genera 52. Ichthyologiae Pars III.—Lugduni Batavorum, Apud Conradum Wishoff. 1738. [iv, 88 pp.]

[v. 4.] Petri Artedi Angermannia-Sueci Synonymia Piscium fere omnium; in qua recensio fit Nominum Piscium, omnium facile Authorum, qui unquam de Piscibus scripsere: nti *Graecorum, Romanorum, Barbarorum*, nec non omnium Insequentium *Ichthyologorum* una cum Nominibus *Inquilinis* variarum nationum. *Opus duo parl.* Ichthyologiae Pars IV.—Lugduni Batavorum, Apud Conradum Wishoff. 1738. [iv, 118, 22 pp.]

[v. 5.] Petri Artedi Sueci Descriptiones Specierum Piscium quas vivos praesertim dissecuit et examinavit, inter quos primario Pisces Regni Sueciae facile omnes accuratissime describuntur cum non paucis aliis exoticis. Ichthyologiae Pars V.—Lugduni Batavorum, Apud Conradum Wishoff. 1738. [iv, 102 pp.]

As indicated in the title of the "Genera Piscium" (v. 3), Artedi admitted into the system 242 nominal species under 52 genera, but in this number are included the Cetaceans, which were regarded as constituting an order of fishes named Plagiuri: these being eliminated (14 species representing 7 genera), the number is reduced to 228 species and 45 genera,—to these, however, may be added 13 other genera indicated by him,—5 in the supplement to the "Genera Piscium," and 8 in the "Synonymia Piscium."

Artedi may be justly regarded as the father of modern ichthyology, having introduced a precise terminology, full and pertinent diagnoses, and throughout uninominal generic names. He first introduced consideration of the number of branchiostegal rays for distinctions of genera, etc. He distributed the true fishes into the orders *Malacopterygii* (=Malacopterygii Cuv.+Syngnathus, Stromateus, Anarrhicas), *Acanthopterygii* (=Acanthopterygii Cuv.), founded on the real or supposed structure of the fins, *Branchiostegii* (a heterogeneous group based on erroneous ideas), and *Chondropterygii* (=Chondropterygii Cuv.)

The edition of the Genera Piscium published by Walbaum (1792) will be noticed under the name of the editor who made the work the vehicle of a new compilation of specific descriptions.

1740-1749.

KLEIN (Jacob Theodor). [1.] Iacobi Theodori Klein Historiae Piscium Naturalis promovendae missus primus de lapillis eorumque numero in craniis piscium, cum praefatione: de piscium auditu. Accesserunt I. Anatome Tur-lanum. II. Observata in capite Raia.—[Motto.] Cum figuris.—Gedani, Litteris Schreiberianis. 1740. [4to, 1 p. l., 36 pp., 5 tab.]

———[2.] Iacobi Theodori Klein Historiae Piscium Naturalis promovendae missus secundus de Piscibus per pulmonibus spirantibus [Cete] ad iustum numerum et ordinem redigendis.—Accesserunt singularia: de I. Dentibus Balaenarum et Elephantium. II. Lapide Manati et Tiburonis.—[Motto]. Cum figuris.—Gedani, Litteris Schreiberianis. 1741. [4to., 3 p. l., 39 pp., 1 L., 6 tab.]

——[3.] Jacobi Theodori Klein Historiae Piscium Naturalis promovendae missus tertius de Piscibus per branchias occultas spirantibus ad justum numerum et ordinem redigendis. Cum observationibus circa partes genitales Rajae maris, et ovarium Galei. [Motto]. Cum figuris.—Gedani, Litteris Schreiberianis. 1742. [4to., 2 p. l., 49 pp., 7 tab.]

——[4.] Jacobi Theodori Klein Historiae Piscium Naturalis promovendae missus quartus de piscibus per branchias apertas spirantibus ad justum numerum et ordinem redigendis. Horum series prima cum additamento ad missum tertium. [Motto]. Cum figuris.—Lipsiae; prostat apud Jo. Frid. Gleditschium ubi & reliqua autoris opuscula. Gedani, Typis Schreiberianis. 1744. [4to., 3 p. l., 68 pp., 15 tab.]

——[5.] Jacobi Theodori Klein Historiae Piscium Naturalis promovendae missus quintus et ultimus de piscibus per branchias apertas spirantibus. Horum series secunda cum additionibus ad missus II, III, IV, et Epistolae de sono piscis carius cavis impacto. [Motto]. Cum figuris.—Gedani, Litteris Schreiberianis. 1749. [4to., 3 p. l., 102 pp., 1 l., 20 tab.]

A remarkable work. It perhaps surpasses all other ichthyological publications in incongruities between the definitions of groups and the contents thereof, and it is difficult to conceive how some could have originated. The definitions themselves are sufficiently clear, and their practical application to forms would not appear to be difficult: the author however seems to have practically ignored his definitions of groups when once framed, and to have proceeded, as some more modern naturalists have done, by successive approximations of other forms to the types of his definitions, and without checking the results by subsequent comparison with the latter. Judging from the character of his various works, his analytical powers appear to have been tolerably fair, but those of synthesis very defective; this defect, an overwhelming exclusiveness of attention to the special subject or idea for the moment under consideration, and a neglect to verify the results afterwards by comparison of all the elements, vitiated his entire work: in addition, he appears to have labored under the disadvantage of an extremely limited autoptical acquaintance with natural objects, a certain stolidity and inaptitude for applying even that little knowledge to the interpretation of figures and descriptions,* and an unbounded trust in the reliability and knowledge of others—except Lund. The stolidity was not sufficiently diluted with unintelligible rhetoric to be entitled profundity.

His classification is a strange one. In the first place, he distributes the fishes (including therewith the cetaceans) into primary groups distinguished (1) by lungs (Cete), or (II) by gills (a) concealed or (b) apparent from the exterior. The true fishes with *concealed gills* were then arranged according to the (1) *position* (lateral or inferior) of the branchial apertures, and (2) the larger sub-division by the presence or absence of (lateral) fins, and finally (3) by the number of branchial apertures. The fishes with externally *visible gills* were distributed into general groups distinguished by positive characters, and the remaining left in one marked by negative characters, —that is, into groups "notable" for some character or other (as to (1), general form; (2), snout; (3), eyes; (4), armature; (5), breast or head; (6), volubility of body).

* For example, he often failed to consider that in symmetrical fishes the lateral fins were double, or present on both sides.

and then enumerated the residuum in which no very salient characters were developed, and whose heterogeneous contents were classified by the number of the fins. But while such was the case theoretically, practically it was quite otherwise, and fancy urged the approximation to the types of his groups of forms on account of supposed resemblances and in forgetfulness of the characters, and which, at another time, under the influence of other ideas, he had referred elsewhere. The nominal species thus scattered, in the several cases, were, however, severally derived from different sources.

A few examples need only be given in demonstration of the truth of these criticisms. The Eels and Leaches (Cobitidae), having the branchial fissures very narrow, were referred to the Fishes with concealed gills, but several species (e. g. Cobitidae, 3 sp.) reappear in the other section under the genus *Enchelyopus*,—the author, overlooking the character of the branchial apertures, having happened to be struck by the resemblance of such forms as were depicted by other authors to certain species for which he had more especially framed the genus: in like manner, species were duplicated under the genera *Enchelyopus* and *Callarias*, *Enchelyopus* and *Laocinus*, and in fact, almost every other genus with numerous species contained some that had been referred elsewhere. In cases like *Mastacembelus*, *Prolisacomus*, and *Solenostomus*, distinguished—one, by the projection of the lower jaw; the second by that of the upper; and the third by the tubular snout, it might be supposed a saliency of character existed which would prevent grossly erroneous references, but it has not detained our author from referring to them species entirely opposed in character. Another mode of procedure is illustrated by the reference of forms to the group distinguished by the "eyes." This was originally suggested by the Heterosomata distinguished by the peculiarity of the two eyes on the same side, but our author has referred to the same (distinguished by the eyes) two combinations of species (*Rhombotides*—Chaetodontidae pp. and *Platiglossa*, related to *Julis*) because, although having no distinctive character whatever in the eyes, he evidently fancied a resemblance between one (*Rhombotides*) and *Rhombus* (Pleuronectidae), and the other (*Platiglossa*) and *Solea*.

The following abstract, selected from his work (Mém. v, p. 00), will give a fuller idea of his system. The incongruity of his genera prevents a comparison with modern types, except in a few cases.

PULMONIBUS spirantes sunt *Physeteræ*. [Cete.] Blaer Mém 11.		
	Dallxcuma concilia Mém III.	*Spiraculis ad latera:* Cynocephalus, Galeus, Pristis, Centracion, Rhina [=Squali]; Batrachus; Crayracion, Capriscus [=Plectognathi]; Conger, Muræna [=Apodes]; Petromyzon. *Spiraculis in thorace:* Narcacion, Rhinobatus, Leiobatus, Dasybatus [=Baiæ].
Pisces		*Formæ:* Balænæ formis. Mém IV. Fasc. i. Silurus. *Rostro:* Fam. II. Acipenser, Latargus [=Anarrhicas], Xiphias, Mastacembelus [=Belone pp.], Paslisantomus, Solenostomus [=Fistularia L. pp.], Amphisilen. *Oculis.* Fasc. III. Solea, Passer, Rhombus, Rhombotides s. Europus, Tetragonopirus, Platiglossa. *Armatura.* Fasc. IV. Cataphractus [=Triglidae pp.], Coristion, Centriscus [=Gasterosteus + Centriscus]. *In sterno & in capite.* Fasc. v. Ostotion [=Cyclopterus], Echeneis.
	Branchius apertis	*Corpore volubili.* Fasc. vi. Enchelyopus.

		TRIPTERUS, *Fam.* vii. Callarias.
		PENTODRTRYPTERUS, *Fasc.* viii. Palamys.
suci notabiles	Pinnis Dorsalibus. *Miss* V.	DIPTERIS, *Fasc.* ix. Trutta, Mullus, Costreus, Lobrax, Sphyraena, Gobio, Asperulus, Asprado, Trichidion.
		PERCOORTTEUS, *Fam.* x. Glaucus, Blennus.
		MONOPTERUS, *Fam.* xi. Perca, Percis, Mormus, Cicla, Synagris, Hipparus, Sargus, Cyprinus, Prochilus, Brama (=Abramis), Mystus, Leuciscus, Harengus, Leuius.
		PERTROMESOPTERUS, *Fasc.* xii. Pseudopterus [= Plarois.]

818 nominal species (exclusive of the Cetaceans) were described under 61 genera, 127 being fishes with concealed gills, 177 having apparent gills and some "notable" feature, and 214 with apparent gills and without notable features.

(1735) 1748–1768.

LINNÉ (Carl von). [1.] Caroli Linnæi, Sueci, Doctoris Medicinæ, Systema Naturæ, sive Regna tria naturæ systematice proposita per classes, ordines, genera, & species.—O Jehova! quam ampla sunt opera Tua! | Quam ea omnia sapienter fecisti! | Quam plena est terra possessione tua! | *Psalm.* civ. 24. | — Lugduni Batavorum, Apud Theodorum Haak. 1735. Ex Typographia Joannis Wilhelmi de Groot. [Fol., 7 ll. unnumbered and unpaged.]

145 species of fishes are enumerated under 36 genera, besides 10 species of Plagiuri (Cete).

The only copy of the original edition, whose existence in the United States is known to me, is in the library of J. Carson Brevoort, Esq., of Brooklyn.

The *third edition*, published in Latin and German by J. J. Lange, at Halle, in 1740, is a reprint of the first.

A textual reprint of the first edition was also published in 1831, viz.:— *Editio prima redita, curante Antonio-Laurentio-Apollinario Fée,* Pharm. Primar. in Schola Medic. Militar. Imolensi; Botanic. Professore, Academ. Medic. Reg. Rosio, etc. [Psalm]— Parisiis, Apud P. G. Levrault, Bibliopolam, via dicta De La Harpe, n. 81. Atque Argentorati, via dicta Des Juifs, n. 33. 1830. [8vo., 2 p. l., vi, 81 pp., 1 l.]

————[2.] Caroli Linnæi Naturæ Curiosorum *Dioscoridis Secundi Systema Naturæ* in quo naturæ regna tria, secundum.[1] Classes, Ordines, Genera, Species, systematice proponuntur. *Editio Secunda, Auctior.*—Stockholmiæ | Apud Gottfr. Kiesewetter. 1740. [8vo., 2 p. l., 80 pp.]

182 species of Fishes are enumerated under 44 genera (83 to 131), besides 8 species of Plagiuri (Cete) under 5 genera.

The *fifth edition* is a reprint of the second, and was published by M. G. Agnethler, at Halle, in 1747 (8vo., 86 pp.); it contains the German names.

————[3.] Caroli Linnæi Medic. & Botan. in Acad. Upsaliensi Professoris Acad. Imperialis, Upsaliensis, Stockholmensis & Montspeliensis Soc. Systema Naturæ in quo proponuntur naturæ regni tria secundum Classes, Ordines, Genera & Species. *Editio quarta ab Auctore emendata & aucta.* Accesserunt nomina Gallica.— Parisiis, Sumptibus Michaelis-Antonii Davidi, bibliopolæ, via Jacobæ, sub signo

Calami antei. 1744. Cum privilegio regis. [8vo., 3 p. l. [Fundamenta Botanica] xxvii, [1,] 108 pp., tab.]

This is said, by Linné, to have been edited by B. Jussieu, and to be the same as the second edition ("per B. Jussieum. Adjecta nomina Gallica. Idem cum 2"). It contains however, in addition to the "Fundamenta Botanica," a special introduction (by himself), which concludes with the remark that it is the *fourth* edition, revised and enlarged (Jam quartam castigatam iterum auctamque Lectori offers Benevole.— p. 3).

238 nominal species of Fishes are enumerated under 48 genera (85 to 129), in addition to the Cetaceans (8 species under 5 genera).

In this edition (and certainly not in the second, as stated by Cuvier), the rays in the fins were also first given for each species.

———[4.] Caroli Linnaei Archiatr. Reg. Med. et Bot. Profess. Upsal. Systema Naturae sistens Regna Tria Naturae, in Classes et Ordines Genera et Species redacta tabulisque aneis illustrata. Cum Privilegio S. R. M. Sveciae & S. R. M. Polonicae ac Electoris Saxon. *Editio sexta, emendata et aucta.*—Stockholmiae. Impensis Godofr. Kiesewetteri 1748. [8vo., iv, 224 pp., 2 p. l., 14 l., 7 pl.]

291 nominal species of Fishes are enumerated, representing 47 genera (102 to 148), and 12 Plagiuri (Cete) representing 6 genera.

The *seventh edition*, published at Leipzig (Lipsiae) in 1748, is a textual reprint of the sixth (Secundum sextam Stockholmiensem emendatam & auctam editionem), by the same publisher, but with the German popular names instead of Swedish.

The *eighth edition* contains the Vegetable Kingdom only.

———[5.] Caroli Linnaei Archiatr. Reg. Med. et Botan. Profess. Upsal. Systema Naturae sistens Regna Tria Naturae in Classes et Ordines Genera et Species redacta tabulisque aneis illustrata. Accedunt vocabula Gallica. *Editio multo auctior & emendatior.*—Lugduni Batavorum, Apud Theodorum Haak, 1756. [8vo., 4 p. l., 227 [+1] pp. [Index], 9 l., 8 pl., with 4 l. explan.]

This edition is recognized by Linné as the *sixth*, and said to have been edited by Gronovius, and to be the same as the sixth, with very few additions respecting the Birds and Fishes. ("Per Gronovium. Panolsrima de Avibus, Piscibus, Mem cum d.") There is, however, a special address to the reader ("Lectori") from the author, in which he acknowledges to have followed the system introduced by Gronovius in the "Museum Ichthyologicum," the first volume of which appeared in 1754 ("Ichthyologiam vero secundum Membranas Branchiostegas & pinnarum radios compendiose tali ordine proponui quali exstat in Gronovii Museo Ichthyologico, cujus mora detecta Genera hac introduxi"). And on comparison, it is found that the sequence of the genera is altogether different from that in the sixth edition, and essentially similar to the one followed by Gronovius: it differs in the following respects:—the sequence of orders is reversed, and the Plagiuri added as the first order: the Chondropterygii different; the sequence in the genera of orders (III) Branchiostegi and (V) Malacopterygii reversed; and the following additional genera incorporated, viz:—113, *Gobius* and 114, *Xiphias* between 112, *Blennius* and 115, *Scomber*; 118, *Ophidion*[*] as the last genus of Acanthopterygii; 144, *Stromateus*, in Malacopterygii, between 143,

———
[*] I have demonstrated, in my memoir on the Atlantics of several doubtful British Fishes (<Proc. Acad. Nat. Sc., Phila., 1861, p. 198, &c.), that *Ophidion* was originally based on the *Ganoid* (*Murenoides* Lac.), and that the *Ophidium imberbe* of Montagu (not Pennant or Lacépède) is the same species.

Anarrhicus and 145, *Pleuronectes*, and 147, *Coryphaena* between 146, *Ammodytes* and 148, *Echeneis*.

236 species of Fishes are enumerated under 38 genera (102 to 159), exclusive of the 13 species of Cetaceans.

————[6.] Caroli Linnaei Equitis De Stella Polari, Archiatri Regii, Med. et Botan. Profess. Upsal.; Acad. Upsal. Holmens. Petropol. Berol. Imper. Lond. Monspel Tolos. Florent. Soc. Systema Naturae per Regna Tria Naturae, secundum Classes, Ordines, Genera, Species, cum Characteribus, Differentiis, Synonymis, Locis. — *Editio Decima, Reformata*. Cum Privilegio S:ae R:ae M:tis Sueciae. — Holmiae, impensis Direct. Laurentii Salvii. 1758 [—] 1759. 8vo., 2 v., viz:—

Tomus I. [Regnum Animale.] 2 p. l., pp. 1-824. 1758.

Tomus II. [Regnum Vegetabile.] 2 p. l., pp. 825-1384. 1759.

In this edition, the binomial system, previously employed by him in the work entitled Museum Tessinianum (1753), was extended in its application to all the kingdoms of nature; the Artedian classification of fishes, adopted in the earlier editions, was superseded by the familiar Linnaean system, and the cetaceans were for the first time eliminated from the class of fishes and grouped with the viviparous quadrupeds under the new class name Mammalia.

A modification of far less merit was the separation of the Chondropterygii of Artedi (exclusive of the genus *Acipenser*) and their combination, under the distinctive term Amphibia Nantes, with the Reptiles. The Fishes thus restricted were distributed into groups distinguished by the supposed structure of the branchiae (Branchiostegi), the want of fins (Apodes), or their presence under the throat (Jugulares), at the thorax (Thoracici), or behind (Abdominales).

414 species of Fishes (including the Amphibia Nantes) were admitted and arranged under 57 genera.

This edition was reproduced at Halle (Halae Magdeburgicae, Typis et Sumptibus Io. Iac. Curt. 1760), in an exact reprint (Praefatus est Ioannes Ioachimus Langius), in 1760, but has not been acknowledged as one of the so-called editions.

The recognised *eleventh edition* was published at Leipzig in 1762, and is also a reprint of the tenth, but was condemned by Linné (Partim prodiit vitiosa. Nil additum).

————[7.] Caroli a Linné, Equitis Aur. de Stella Polari, Archiatri Regii, Med. & Botan. Profess. Upsal., Acad. Paris. Upsal. Holmens. Petropol. Berol. Imper. Lond. Angl. Monspel. Tolos. Florent. Edinb. Bern. Soc. Systema Naturae per Regna Tria Naturae, secundum Classes, Ordines, Genera, Species, cum Characteribus, Differentiis, Synonymis, Locis. Tomus I(—) III. — *Editio Duodecima, Reformata*. Cum Privilegio S:ae R:ae M:tis Sueciae & Electoris Saxon. — Holmiae, Impens. Direct. Laurentii Salvii, 1766 [—] 1768. [8vo., 3 v., viz:—

Tomus I. [Regnum Animale.—Pars 1: Mammalia. Aves. Amphibia. Pisces. pp. 1-532. 1766. Pars 2: Insecta. Vermes. 1 p. l., pp. 533-1328, 11 l. 1767.]

Tomus II. [Regnum Vegetabile. 736 pp., 8 l.] 1767.

" III. [Regnum Lapideum.—Appendix Animalium. Appendix Vegetabilium. 236 pp., 10 l. 3 pl. folded.] 1768.

The last edition published by Linné.

The class Pisces was in this edition further restricted by the exclusion of the Branchiostegi of Artedi (including the dismembered genera *Tetrodon* and *Diodon*), and the genera *Centriscus*, *Syngnathus*, and *Pegasus* from the Fishes and their conjunction with the forms rejected in the tenth edition and the combination of all under the Amphibia Nantes, which were subdivided into two groups distinguished by the separated branchial chambers (Spiraculis compositis) or single apertures (Spiraculis solitariis).

477 nominal species of Fishes (including the Amphibia Nantes) were described, and referred to 61 genera. The additional genera were *Amia*, *Elops* (both founded for fishes sent by Dr. Garden from South Carolina), *Cepola*, and *Teuthis*.

In conclusion, it may be said that the original editions recognised by Linné as completely revised ones were the *first* (1735), the *second* (1740), the *sixth* (1748), the *tenth* (1758), and the *twelfth* (1766–68).

The first was reprinted at Halle, in 1740, and the reprint recognised as the *third*: and again at Paris in 1830.

The second was reprinted at Paris, in 1744 (with modifications), as the *fourth* edition; and at Halle, in 1747, and the reissue was subsequently recognised as the *fifth* edition.

The sixth edition was reissued at Leipsig, and subsequently known as the *seventh*; and closely followed in the edition of Leipsig, recognised as the *ninth*.

The eighth edition did not contain the Animal Kingdom.

The tenth edition was reproduced at Halle in 1760 (not recognised), and at Leipsig in 1762, the last being acknowledged as the *eleventh*.

The *twelfth edition* was reprinted at Vienna, in 1767–70, and entitled the *thirteenth*, but is not esteemed as one of the regular current editions.

The later *thirteenth edition*, in which Gmelin brought together descriptions of species unrecognized by Linné and unknown to him, is noticed under the editor's name (1788).

1770.

GOÜAN (Antoine). Historia Piscium, sistens ipsorum Anatomen externam, internam, atque Genera in Classes & Ordines redacta. Accedunt Vocabularium completissimum, Indices latini ac gallici, Experimenta circa Motum natatorium & muscularem, Respirationis mechanismum, Auditus & Generationis organa. Cum iconibus Genera nova ac præcipuas partes Anatomicas exhibentibus. Auctore Antonio Goüan, Regis Consiliario et Medico ordinario, Professore Regio in Ludoviceo Monspeliensi, Societ. regiæ Scient. Monspel. Sodali, regiæ Scient. Humaniorum Litterarum et Inscriptionum Tolosanæ Correspondenti, Academiæ Botanicæ Florentinæ Socio honorario.—Argentorati, Sumptibus Amandi König, bibliopolæ, 1770. Cum privilegio Regis.—

or,

Histoire des Poissons, contenant la Description Anatomique de leurs parties externes & internes, & le caractère des divers Genres rangés par Classes & par Ordres. Avec un Vocabulaire complet, des Tables raisonnées en latin & en français, des Expériences sur le Mouvement natatoire et musculaire, sur le méchanisme de la Respiration, sur les organes de l'Ouïe et de la Génération, & des Estampes qui représentent les principales parties anatomiques à quelques Genres nouveaux. Par M. Antoine Goüan, ...—à Strasbourg, chez Amand König, libraire. 1770. Avec privilège du Roi. [4to., xviii (doubled), 252 (1–228 doubled) + [3] pp., 4 pl. folded.]

The text is in both Latin and French, corresponding on opposite pages.

The title of this work is misleading, as only the *Genera* of fishes are described. The modifications introduced into the class by Linné in the tenth edition of the *Systema Naturæ* (the exclusion of the *Chondropterygii*, less *Aripenser* and with the addition of *Lophius*, and their union with the *Amphibia*) are adopted. Thus limited, the genera are (1) combined according to the Artedian system, and (2) those combinations then subdivided, with Linné, into groups distinguished by the want or position of the ventral fins. The genera were quite well described, and three new ones still retained in the System (*Lepadogaster*, *Lepidopus*, and *Trachypterus*) were established.

1782–1795.

BLOCH (Mark Eliæser). D. Marcus Eliæser Bloch's, . . . , ausübenden Arztes zu Berlin, Oekononomische Naturgeschichte der Fische Deutschlands. [Text, 4to.; Pl., obl. fol., 3 v. viz:—

  [1.] Mit sieben und dreissig Kupfertafeln nach Originalen. Erster Theil.— Berlin, 1782. Auf Kosten des Verfassers und in Commission bei dem Buchhändler Hr. Hesse. [8 p. l., 258 pp.]

  [2.] Mit fünf und dreissig Kupfertafeln nach Originalen. Zweiter Theil.— Berlin, 1783. Auf Kosten des Verfassers und in Commission in der Buchhandlung der Realschule. [4 pl., 192 pp.]

  [3.] Mit sechs und dreissig ausgemalten Abdrücken nach Originalen und einem Titelkupfer. Dritter Theil. [=v. 2. 1784.]

  The text is in 4to.; the plates, in fol., without special titles.

——— D. Marcus Eliæser Bloch's, ausübenden Arztes zu Berlin, ... Naturgeschichte der ausländischen Fische. [Text, 4to.; Pl., obl. fol., 9 v. viz:—

  [4.] Mit sechs und dreissig ausgemalten Kupfern nach Originalen. — Erster Theil. Berlin, 1785. Auf Kosten des Verfassers, und in Commission in der Buchhandlung der Realschule. [viii, 136 pp.]

  [5.] [=v. 4.] Zweiter Theil. Berlin 1786. [=v. 4.—viii, 160 pp.]

  [6.] Mit sechs und dreissig ausgemalten Kupfern nach Originalen und einem Titelkupfer. Dritter Theil. Berlin 1787. [=v. 4, 5.—xiv, 146 pp.]

  [7.] Mit sechs und dreissig Ausgemalten Kupfern nach originalen. Vierter Theil. Berlin 1790. Bey den Königl. Akademischen Kunsthändlern J. Morino & Comp. [xii, 128 pp.]

  [8.] [=v. 7.] Fünfter Theil. Berlin 1791. [=v. 7—viii, 152 pp.]

  [9.] [=v. 7, 8.] Sechster Theil. Berlin 1792. [=v. 7, 8.—xii, 126 pp.]

  [10.] [=v. 7–9.] Siebenter Theil. Berlin 1793. [=v. 7–9.—xiv, 144 pp.]

  [11.] [=v. 7–10.] Achter Theil. Berlin 1794. [v. 7–10.—vi, 174 pp.]

  [12.] Mit sechs und dreissig Ausgemalten Abdrücken nach Originalen. Neunter Theil. Berlin 1795. Im Verlage der Morinoschen Kunsthandlung. [iv, 192 pp.]

The nine parts of the last work (Natural History of Foreign Fishes) were complementary to the first (Economical History of the Fishes of Germany), and together formed a uniform series, afterwards entitled:—

Allgemeine Naturgeschichte der Fische.

The three volumes of the first work formed volumes I to III of the collection, and the nine of the last, volumes IV to XII.

November, 1872. 6

—— Icthyologie, ou Histoire Naturelle, générale et particulière des Poissons.
Avec des figures enluminées, dessinées d'après nature. Par Marc Eliéser
Bloch. · · · · [Fol., 12 v., viz :—

[1e Série.]

[1.] Première partie. Avec 37 planches.—À Berlin, chez l'auteur, et chez
François de la Garde libraire, 1785. [5 p. l., 206 pp., 1 l., pl. 1-37.]

[2.] Seconde partie. Avec 35 planches.—[=v. 1.] 1785. [1 title, 170 pp.,
1 l., pl. 38-72.]

[3.] Troisième partie. Avec 34 planches.—[=v. 2.] 1786. [1 p. l., 160 pp.,
1 l., pl. 73-107.]

[4.] Quatrième partie. Avec 36 planches.
   À Berlin,   ⎞   ⎛ l'Auteur, à † chez François de la Garde libraire.
   À Paris,   ⎬ chez ⎨ Didot le jeune, · · · ·
   À Londres,   ⎠   ⎝ White & Fils, · · · · 1787.
   [1 p. l., 134 pp., 1 l., pl. 108-144.]

[5.] Cinquième partie. Avec 36 planches.—[=v. 4.] 1787. [1 p. l., 130 pp.,
1 l., pl. 145-180.]

[6.] Sixième et dernière partie. Avec trente-six planches.—[=v. 4, 5.] 1788.
[1 p. l. viii, 150 pp., 1 l., pl. 181-216.]

[2e Série.]

[7.] Septième partie. Avec 35 planches.—À Berlin, chez l'Auteur.—À Leipzig
dans la Musée de Mr. Boygang et chez tous les libraires d'Allemagne,
1797. [1 p. l. viii, 104 pp., 1 l., pl. 217-252.]

[8.] Huitième partie. Avec 36 planches.—[=v. 7.] 1797. [1 p. l. iv, 122
pp., 1 l., pl. 253-288.]

[9.] Neuvième partie. Avec 36 planches.—[=v. 7, 8.] 1797. [1 p. l., 110
pp., 1 l., pl. 289-324.]

[10.] Dixième partie. Avec 36 planches.—[=v. 7-9.] 1797. [1 p. l., v, 130
pp., 1 l., pl. 325-360.]

[11.] Onzième partie. Avec 36 planches.—[=v. 7-10.] 1797. [2 p. l., 136
pp., 1 l., pl. 361-396.]

[12.] Douzième partie. Avec 36 planches.—[=v. 7-11.] 1797. [1 p. l. ll,
142 pp., 2 l., pl. 397-432.]

A translation, by Laveau, of the preceding series.

A cheap edition of this work was published in "Suites à Buffon" (v. 32-41), with
the plates of Bloch, copied and reduced by J. E. Deseve, and under the following
title :—

—— Histoire Naturelle des Poissons, avec les figures dessinées d'après nature par
Bloch. Ouvrage classé par ordres, genres et espèces, d'après le système de
Linné; avec les caractères génériques ; par René Richard Castel, · · · ·
Second édition.—À Paris, chez Déterville, · · · · an X, [1802. 12mo, 10 v.,
with 160 pl. 3e éd. Roret, 1837.—20 fr. 20c.; col. 67 fr.]

1787.

HAÜY (René Just). Encyclopédie Méthodique.—Histoire Naturelle. Tome troisième. Contenant les ·Poissons. [Anon.]—À Paris, chez Panckoucke, libraire,
· · · · À Liège, chez Plomteux, imprimeur des États. 1787 · · · · [4to, 2
p. l. lx, 435 pp.]

This is a dictionary, in which the Linnean orders (miscalled classes of orders), genera, and species are described under their French names in alphabetical order. Tabular synopses (each on a special page) are also given of the classes, genera, and species under their French names, in connection with the descriptions. The work is a very poor and imperfect compilation, by an author practically unacquainted with Fishes as well as with the then recent literature of the subject. The following is a complement to it:—

1788.

BONNATERRE (J . . . P . . .). Tableau Encyclopédique et Méthodique des trois règnes de la Nature, dédié et présenté à M. Necker, Ministre d'Etat, & Directeur général des Finances. — Ichtyologie. — Par M. l'Abbé Bonnaterre. . . . , —A Paris, chez Panckoucke, libraire, ... 1788. . . . . [4to, vi, 215 pp., 3 (A, B) +100 pl.]

A poor compilation, arranged according to the Linnean classification, by an individual who was employed by Panckoucke, the publisher of the Encyclopédie Méthodique, to bring together the illustrations of the Mammals, Birds, Reptiles, Fishes, and Insects. The compiler has availed himself of the works of most of the authors preceding, and collected illustrations of more than 400 species.

1788.

GMELIN (Johann Friedrich). Caroli a Linné, Equitis auratī de stella polari, Archiatri Regii, Med. et Botan. Profess. Upsal. Acad. Paris. Upsal. Holm. Petropol. Berolin. Imper. Londin. Angl. Monsp. Tolos. Florent. Edinb. Bern. Soc. Systema Naturae per regna tria Naturae, secundum Classes, Ordines, Genera, Species, cum characteribus, differentiis, synonymis, locis. Tomus I. [—] III. Editio Decima tertia, Aucta, Reformata. Cura Jo. Fred. Gmelin, Philos. et Med. Doctor. Hujus et Chem. in Georgia Augusta Prof. P. O. Acad. Caesar. Naturae Curiosorum et Electoral. Moguntin. Erfordensis, nec non Societ. Reg. Scient. Gottingensis, Physicae Tigurin., et Metallicae Membri.—Lipsiae, 1788 -93. Impensis Georg. Emanuel. Beer. [8vo, 4120 pp., 3 v. in 9 parts, viz:—

The three volumes, being very much amplified, were divided into parts, with half titles, for binding, viz:—

> Tomus I. [Regnum Animale: pars I. (Mammalia; Aves, ordines 1–2), 6 p.l., pp. 1–500: pars II. (Aves, ordines 3–8), 1 p.l., pp. 501–1032: pars III. (Amphibia, Pisces), 1 p.l., pp. 1033 (Pisces, 1126)–1516: pars iv. (Insecta, ordines 1–2), 1 p.l., pp. 1517–2224: pars v. (Insecta, ordines 3–7), 1 p.l., pp. 2225–3020: pars vi. (Vermes), 1 p.l., pp. 3021–3910: pars vii. (Indices), 1 p.l., pp. 3911–4120.] 1789.
>
> Tomus II. [Regnum Vegetabile:] pars I., 1 p.l. al, 884 pp. : pars II., 1 p.l., pp. 885–1661.] 1791.
>
> Tomus III. [Regnum Lapidenm.] 476 pp., 3 pl. folded. 1793.

This edition is noticed under the date of 1788 and the name of Gmelin, as that naturalist is alone responsible for the incorporation of the many species described since the last edition of the Systema Naturae revised by Linné. The compilation displays very little acquaintance with any branch of Zoology, and species are incorporated into the system in defiance of the characters of the groups to which they are referred. This is evidently the result of blind confidence in the accuracy and powers of dissemination of those whose species were incorporated by him into the System, as he did not hesitate to adopt their views as to generic relations, however much the inherent evidence of their own descriptions might oppose their views. A large number of the species were thus repeated under different specific as well as generic names. The number of nominal species was thereby increased to 820, grouped under 65 genera, (150a) *Sternoptyx*, (154b) *Leptocephalus*, (155a) *Kurtus*, (165a) *Scarus*, and (170a) *Centrogaster* having been added to the Linnean genera. Gmelin, however, improved on the Linnean system by the re-combination of the Amphibia nantes with the Pisces, and he re-adopted the orders (V) Branchiostegi and (VI) Chondropterygii. He erred, on the other hand, in separating *Mormyrus* from the Abdominales and referring it to the Branchiostegi.

1792.

WALBAUM (Johann Julius). Petri Artedi Sueci Genera Piscium. In quibus Systema totum Ichthyologiae proponitur cum classibus, ordinibus, generum characteribus, specierum differentiis, observationibus plurimis. Redactis speciebus 242 [228] ad Genera 62 [45]. Ichthyologiae Pars III. — Emendata et aucta a Iohanne Iulio Walbaum, M.D., Societatis Berolinensis Naturae Curiosorum, et Societatis Litterariae Lubecensis Sodali. Cum tabula aenea. —Grypeswaldiae, impensis Ant. Ferdin. Röse 1792. [8vo., 4 p. l., 723 pp., 3 pl.]

A poor compilation, like Gmelin's, in which the various previously described species were introduced without a critical study into the system, and described in foot-notes in connection with the Artedian species, but combined under the Linnean genera. The nominal species (and many are only nominal), excluding the cetaceans, are thus raised from 228 to about 965, without counting the species enumerated under the new genera of authors appended to the volume. The compilation has some value, not only on account of the original descriptions of species copied from previous authors, but because of the reproductions of the descriptions of the new genera introduced by various authors into the system. It is also of interest to the student of American species by reason of the incorporation therein, under specific names, of anonymous American species described by Schœpf.

1798–1803.

LACÉPÈDE (Bernard Germain Étienne de la Ville-sur-Illon, Comte de). Histoire Naturelle des Poissons, [v. 1] par le citoyen La Cépède, membre de l'Institut national, et Professeur du Muséum de histoire naturelle. Tome premier [–5]. —A Paris, chez Plassan, imprimeur libraire, Rue du Cimetière André-des-Arcs, No. 10. L'An VI de la République. —1798. [—L'an XI de la République, i. e., 1803] [4to., 5 v.]

The title-page was modified in each volume, and the personal titles successively increased in number; the address of the publisher was changed (in v. 3–5); the last volume (on title-page) was dedicated to his late wife; and only the first volume bears the date of the Christian era.

Originally published and frequently reproduced in connection with Buffon's works, e. g., Buffon, 1st ed. (1749–84), v. 39–43 ; 1st 12mo. ed. (1752–1805), v. 78–88 ; Lacépède's 1st ed. (1799–1803), 14 v. ; Lacépède's 2d ed. (1817–19), v. 13–17 ; Lamouroux and Desmarest's ed. (1824–32), suite—i. e., Œuvres du Comte de Lacépède—v. 5–11 ; Larcin's ed. (1829–34), about 25 v. ; also, republished in "Histoire Naturelle" (Furne et c°), in 1855 ; the compilation ascribed to Sonnini DE MANONCOUR

(Charles Nicolas Sigisbert) is also merely a slightly modified reprint of the same work. The last is entitled: Histoire Naturelle générale et particulière des Poissons; ouvrage faisant Suite à l'Histoire Naturelle, générale et particulière; composée par Leclerc de Buffon, et mise dans un nouvel ordre [v. 9, 10, 11, "Rédige"] par C. S. Sonnini, avec des notes et additions. Par C. S. Sonnini, - - - -.—Paris, de l'imprimérie de F. Dufart, an XI [—] XII [1803-1805—8vo., 13 vols.]

A work by an able man and eloquent writer (even prone to aid rhetoric by the aid of the imagination, in absence of desirable facts), but which, on account of undue confidence in others, default of comparison of materials from want thereof and otherwise, and carelessness generally, is entirely unreliable. Many species appear under several different names, and in genera widely separated. The classification adopted is a progressiau system of (1) subclasses, (2) divisions, and (3) orders.

First, Subclasses, based on the supposed consistence of the skeleton (Sonsclasses (1) Poissons cartilagineux ; (2) Poissons osseux).

Second, Divisions, under each subclass, established on the supposed presence or absence and various combinations (4) of the opercula and branchiostegal membrane, that is, the presence of both ; of one ; or, the other ; or, none.

Third, Orders, distinguished by the absence of ventrals (Apodes), or their presence at different regions (Jugulaires, Thoracieu, Abdominaux).

Several of these categories are non-existent in nature, and the reference of species to them is due to erroneous observation or supposition.

Fourteen hundred and sixty-three (1463) nominal species were described.

<h2 style="text-align:center">1801.</h2>

BLOCH (Marc Elieser), and Johann Gottlob **SCHNEIDER.** M. E. Blochii, Doctoris Medicinae Berolinensis, et societatibus literariis multis descripti, Systema Ichthyologiae iconibus cx illustratum. Post obitum auctoris opus inchoatum absolvit, correxit, interpolavit Jo. Gottlob Schneider, Saxo.—Berolini, sumtibus auctoris impressum et bibliopolio Sanderiano commissum. 1801. [8vo., lx, 584 pp., 110 col. pl.]

A compilation in which the various species described by authors are collected together, and referred with very little judgment to the genera admitted. The class is arranged in a new manner, avowedly according to the number of the fins, but very frequently in defiance of their true number and morphology, as notably in the genera 1, 2, 4, 7, 21, 37, 38, but, also, in very many others. The system is as follows, the genera described as new (in Bloch's previous works as well as the present) being indicated by italics :—

Classis I. Hendecapterygii. (11 fins.)—1. *Lepadogaster.*

Classis II. Decapterygii. (10 fins.)
Ordo I. Jugulares.—2. Gadus.
Ordo II. Thoracici.—3. Trigla.
Ordo III. Abdominales.—4. *Polynemus.*

Classis III. Enneapterygii. (9 fins.)—5. Scomber.

Classis IV. Octopterygii. (8 fins.)
Ordo I. Jugulares.—6. *Callionymus*; 7. Batrachus; 8. Uranoscopus; 9. *Eurichyopus*; 10. Trachinus; 11. *Phycis.*
Ordo II. Thoracici.—12. Platycephalus; 13. Cottus; 14. Periophthalmus; 15. Eleotris; 16. Gobius; 17. *Jadsius*; 18. Mullus; 19. Sciaena; 20. Perca; 21. Xiphias; 22. Zeus; 23. Brama; 24. *Monocentris*; 25. *Lomborus*; 26. Macrurus; 27. *Ayseus*; 28. Equas.

Ordo III. Abdominales. — 29. *Cataphractus* (=Callichthys); 30. Sphyrænæ; 31. Atherina; 32. Centriscus; 33. Fistularia; 34. Mugil; 35. Oxalerostlana; 36. Loricaria; 37. Squalus.

Classis V. Heptapterygii. (7 fins.)

Ordo I. Jugulares.—38. Lophius; 39. Piorsellis; 40. Pleuronectes; 41. *Kyrtes*; 42. *Trichogaster*; 43. *Centronotus* (=Murænoides); 44. Blennius; 45. *Percis*; 46. Trichonotus.

Ordo II. Thoracici.—47. *Monoceros*; 48. *Grammistes*; 49. Scorpæna; 50. *Synancia*; 51. Cyclopterus; 52. *Amphiprion*; 53. *Amphacanthus* (=Teuthis, L.); 54. Acanthurus; 55. Chætodon; 56. *Alphestes*; 57. *Ophicephalus* (Bl. Aml. Fischo, viii); 58. Lepidopus; 59. Echeneis; 60. Cepola; 61. Labrus; 62. Sparus; 63. Scarus; 64. Coryphæna; 65. *Epinephelus*; 66. *Anthias*; 67. *Cephalophalis*; 68. Callidon; 69. Holocentrus; 70. *Lutianus*; 71. *Bodianus*; 72. *Cichla*; 73. *Gymnocephalus*.

Ordo III. Abdominales.—74. Acipenser; 75 Chimæra; 76. Pristis; 77. *Rhina*; 78. Rhinobatus; 79. Raja; 80. *Platystacus*; 81. Silurus; 82. Anableps; 83. *Acanthonotus* (=Notacanthus); 84. Esox; 85. Synodus; 86. Salmo; 87. Clupea; 88. Exocoetus; 89. *Clariodus*; 90. Elops; 91. Albula; 92. Cobitis; 93. Cyprinus; 94. Amia; 95. *Poecilia*; 96. Pegasus; 97. Mormyrus; 98. Polyodon; genus dubium 99. Argentina.

Classis VI. Hexapterygii. (6 fins.)

[Ordo I.] Apodes.—100. Balistes; 101. *Ryuchobdella*.

Ordo II. Pinna anali carentes.—102. Trachypterus; 103. *Gymnetrus* (=Regalecus Brunn).

Classis VII. Pentapterygii. (Fins 5.)

Ordo I. Apodes.—104. Ophidium; 104a. Pomatias; 104b. *Gunthobolus* (= Odontognathus Lac.); 105. Muræna; 106. Stromateus; 107. Ammodytes; 108. Sternoptyx; 109. Amarhicas; 110. *Chœna*; 111. *Sternorchus*; 112. Ostracion; 113. Tetrodon; 114. *Orthragoriscus*; 115. Diodon; 116. Syngnathus.

Classis VIII. Tetrapterygii. Apodes.—117. Trichiurus; 118. *Bogmarus* (=Trachypterus Ocan); 118a. Tænoides; 119. Stylephorus.

Classis IX. Tripterygii.

Ordo I. Apodes.—120. Gymnonotus.

Ordo II. Achiri et Apodes. — 121. *Synbranchus*; 122. *Gymnothorax* (=Muræna L.).

Classis X. Dipterygii.

Ordo I. Apodes.—123. Orca.

Ordo II. Apodes et Achiri.—124. Petromyzon; 125. Leptocephalus.

Classis XI. Monopterygii. Apodes et Achiri.—126. *Gastrobranchus* (=Myxine Linn.); 127. *Sphagebranchus* (=Ophichthys Ahl.); 127a. *Fluta* (= Monopterus Lac.); 128. *Typhlobranchus*.

1803-1804.

SHAW (George). General Zoology or Systematic Natural History. By George Shaw, M.D., F.R.S., &c., with plates from the first authorities and most select specimens, engraved principally by Mr. Heath. — [Specifications.] — London: [v. 1-7,] Printed for G. Kearsley, Fleet Street. [v. 8-14, by others]. 1800 [—] 1826. [8vo., 14 v.]

Besides the engraved title, copied above, there is, on the following leaf, a short printed one, viz.:—General Zoology.—[Specifications.]—London: [Publishers]. —1800 [—] 1826. The later volumes were by James Francis Stephenson.

The ichthyological portion is contained in the fourth and fifth volumes, viz:—

Vol. IV. Part I. Pisces.— . . . . . 1803. [1 eng. title, 1 plain title, pp. v, [1,] 1-186, pl. 1-25.—*Apodes* 33 sp.; *Jugulares*, 53 sp.=100 sp.]

Vol. IV. Part II. Pisces.— . . . . 1803. [1 eng. title, pp. xi, [+41], incl. pl. title, 187-632, pl. 26-92+43, 65, 69, 74.— *Thoracici*, 672 sp.]

Vol. V. Part I. Pisces.— . . . . 1804. [1 eng. title, 1 pl. title, pp. v, [+iii,] 1-250, pl. 93-132.— *Abdominales*, 261 sp.]

Vol. V. Part II. Pisces.— . . . . 1804. [1 eng. title, pp. vi, [+ii.] incl. pl. title, 251-463, pl. 133-182+158.—*Cartilaginei*, 191 sp.]

This part is a compilation, based on the system of Linné as modified by Gmelin in the restoration of the Amphibia nantes to the Fishes. It is even worse than its predecessors in the incorporation of species unknown to Linné! In the genera. The illustrations are almost entirely copied from the works of Bloch and Lacépède, only five or six (according to Cuvier), representing species in the British Museum, being original. Two new generic types (*Trachichthys* and *Stylophorus*) are added, one of which, however (*Trachichthys*), had been previously described in the Naturalists' Miscellany (v. X).

Twelve hundred and thirty (1230) nominal species were described.

The generic diagnoses, it may be added, were copied (sometimes with very slight modifications) by Dr. S. L. Mitchill in his memoir ("The Fishes of New York, described and arranged") in the "Transactions of the Literary and Philosophical Society of New York."

1828–1849.

CUVIER (Georges Chrétien Léopold Dagobert, baron) and Achille **VALENCIENNES**. Histoire naturelle des poissons, par M. le Bⁿ Cuvier, . . . ; et par M. Valenciennes, ... Tome premier [—Tome vingt-deuxième.]—— À Paris, [v. 1-12] chez F. G. Levrault, ... 1828 [-37]; [v. 13-14], chez Pitois-Levrault et Cⁱ, ... 1839; [v. 15] ; chez Ch. Pitois, éditeur, . . . 1840; [v. 16-22] chez P. Bertrand, (etc.). 1842-1849.

As indicated on the reverse of the bastard title, all the volumes were printed at Strasbourg, v. 1 to 13 having been printed by F. G. Levrault (Imprimerie de F. G. Levrault), and v. 14 to 22 by the widow Levrault. (Imprimerie de Vᵉ Berger-Levrault.)

CONTENTS.

v. 1. Livre premier.—Tableau historique des progrès de l'ichtyologie, depuis son origine jusqu'à nos jours.

Livre deuxième.—Idée générale de la nature et de l'organisation des poissons. 1828.

v. 2-3. Livre troisième.—Des poissons de la famille des Perches, ou des Percoïdes. [Par Cuvier.] 1828-29.

v. 4. Livre quatrième.—Des acanthoptérygiens à joue cuirassée. [Par Cuvier.] 1829.

v. 5. Livre cinquième.—Des Sciénoïdes. [Par Cuvier.] 1830.

v. 6. Livre sixième.—(Partie I. Des Sparoïdes; Partie II. Des Ménides.) 1830. [Par Cuvier et Valenciennes.]

v. 7. Livre septième.—Des Squamipennes. [Par Cuvier?] Livre huitième.—Des poissons à pharyngiens labyrinthiformes. 1831. [Par Cuvier?]

v. 8-9. Livre neuvième. Des Scombéroïdes. 1831-33. [Par Cuvier et Valenciennes.]

v. 10. Suite du l. 9.—Des Scombéroïdes. [Par Cuvier et Valenciennes?] Livre dixième.—De la famille des Teuthies. [Par Cuvier et Valenciennes?] " onzième.—De la famille des Teuthoïdes. [Par Cuvier et Valenciennes!] " douzième.—Des Athérines. 1835. [Par Cuvier et Valenciennes?]

v. 11. Livre treizième.—Des Mugiloïdes. Livre quatorzième.—De la famille des Gobioïdes. 1836.

v. 12. Suite du livre quatorzième.—Gobioïdes. Livre quinzième.—Des acanthoptérygiens à pectorales pédiculées. 1837.

v. 13. Livre seizième.—Labroïdes. 1839.

v. 14. Suite du livre seizième.—Labroïdes. Livre dix-septième.—Des Malacoptérygiens. Des Siluroïdes. 1839.

v. 15. Suite du livre dix-septième.—Siluroïdes. 1840.

v. 16-17. Livre dix-huitième.—Cyprinoïdes. 1842.

v. 18. Suite du livre dix-huitième.—Cyprinoïdes. Livre dix-neuvième.—Des Ésoces ou Lucioïdes. 1846.

v. 19. Suite du livre dix-neuvième.—Brochets ou Lucioïdes. Livre vingtième.—De quelques familles* de Malacoptérygiens, intermédiaires entre les Brochets et les Clupes. 1846.

v. 20. Livre vingt et unième.—De la famille des Clupéoïdes. 1847.

v. 21. Suite du livre vingt et unième et des Clupéoïdes.† 1848. Livre vingt-deuxième.—De la famille des Salmonoïdes.

v. 22. Suite du livre vingt-deuxième.—Suite de la famille des Salmonoïdes. 1849.

Two editions were published, one in octavo and the other in quarto, but from the same types, adjusted only for difference of form. Of each edition, copies with colored and uncolored plates were published; the price of the octavo edition with plain plates was, for the first twelve volumes, 13 francs 50 centimes per volume, afterwards (v. 13-22), 18 francs 50 centimes; with colored plates, 23 francs 50 centimes, afterwards raised to 39 francs 50 centimes; of the quarto edition with plain plates, at first 18 francs, and afterwards (v. 13-22), 28 francs; with colored plates, 18 francs, afterwards 48 francs per volume. For sets in octavo with plain plates, 300 (Grässe) or 429 (Lorenz) francs, and with colored plates, 600 (Grässe) or 869 (Lorenz) francs; in quarto with plain plates, 430 (Grässe) or 616 (Lorenz) francs, and with colored plates, 800 (Grässe) or 1056 (Lorenz) francs.

* The families referred to are: Chirocentres (with the genus Chirocentrus), Alepocéphales (with Alepocephalus), Lutodeires (with Chanos and Gonorhynchus), Mormyres (with Mormyrus), Hyodontes (with Osteoglossum, Pachenormus, and Myodon), Butirins (with Albulaus Butirinus) Elopies (with Elops and Megalopus), Amies (with Amia), Tarpons ou Amies? (Vastres), familia particuliere, ou Amies? (Sterolis), Erythrinides (with Erythrinus, Macrodon, Lebiarina, and Pyrrhulina), and Ombres (with Umbra).

† The Xiopteres are discriminated from the Clupeides as a very distinct family (une famille très distincte).

v. 1. xvi, 574 pp. 1 l.   xiv, 422 pp. 1 L   pl. 1–8 [double].   1828.*
   2. xxi, [1 l.] 490 pp.   xvii, [1 l.] 371 pp.   pl. 9–40.   1828.
   3. xxviii, 500 pp. 1 l.   xxii, [1 l.] 368 pp.   pl. 41–71.   1829.
   4. xxvi, [1 l.] 518 pp.   xx, [1 l.] 379 pp.   pl. 72–99, 97 bis.   1829.
   5. xxviii, 490 pp. 2 l.   xx, 374 pp. 2 l.   pl. 100–140.   1830.
   6. xxiv, 559 pp. 3 L   xviii, [3 l.] 470 pp.   pl. 141–169, 162 bis, 162 ter,
                                                    162 quater, 167 bis, 168 bis.
   7. xxix, 531 pp. 3 l.   xxii, [3 l.] 399 pp.   pl. 170–208.   1831.
   8. xix, [2 l.] 509 pp.   xe, [2 l.] 375 pp.   pl. 209–245.   1831.
   9. xxia, 512 pp. 1 l.   xxiv, [1 l.] 379 pp.   pl. 246–279.   1833.
  10. xxiv, 492 pp. 1 l.   xix, [1 l.] 358 pp.   pl. 280–306.   1835.
  11. xx, 506 pp. 1 l.   xv, [1 l.] 373 pp.   pl. 307–343.   1836.
  12. xxiv, 507 + 1 pp.   xx, 377 pp. 1 l.   pl. 344–368.   1837.
  13. xix, 505 pp. 1 l.   xvii, 370 pp.   pl. 369–388.   1839.
  14. xvii, 464 pp. 3 l.   xx, 344 pp. 3 L   pl. 389–420.   1839.
  15. xxxi, 540 pp. 1 l.   xxiv, 397 pp.   pl. 421–455.   1840.
  16. xv, 172 pp. 1 L   xviii, 363 pp. 1 l.   pl. 456–487.   1842.
  17. xxiii, 497 pp. 1 L   xx, 370 pp. 1 l.   pl. 497 [bis]–519.   1844.
  18. xix, 505 pp. 2 l.   xviii, 375 pp. 2 L   pl. 520–553.   1846.
  19. xix, 544 pp. 3 l.   xv, 391 pp. 2 L   pl. 554–590.   1846.
  20. xviii, 472 pp. 1 l.   xiv, 346 pp. 1 L   pl. 591–606.   1847.
  21. xiv, 536 pp.   xiii [+ lii], 391 pp.   pl. 607–633.   1848.
  22. xx, 532, 91(+1) pp. xvi, 395, [index] 61+1 pp. pl. 634–650.   1849.

4514] nominal species were described in the 22 volumes: all belonging to the order
Teleocephali, except the Gasterosteidae (17 sp.), Opisthomi (sp.), Nematognathi
(218 sp.), Scyphophori (12 sp.), and Aroididae (10 sp.), to balance which the Cichlidae (or Chromididae), Ananthini and Gymnarchidae almost alone remained to be
described.

Complementary. 1865–1870.

DUMÉRIL (August). 'Histoire naturelle des Poissons ou Ichthyologie générale
par Aug. Duméril [,] professeur-administrateur au Muséum d'Histoire naturelle
de Paris.—Ouvrage accompagné de planches.—[See "contents."]—Paris [,]
Librairie encyclopédique de Roret, · · · · 1865. [–]1870. [Text 8vo. Atlas,
larger 8vo.]

contents.

Tome premier [.] Elasmobranches [i. e.] Plagiostomes et Holocéphales ou Chi-
mères.—Première partie. · · · 1865. [2 p. l. pp. 1–352]; Seconde partie.
· · · 1865. [2 p. l. pp. 353–720.—With atlas, 10 fr.; col., 19 fr.]

Tome second [.] Ganoïdes, Dipnés, Lophobranches. · · · 1870. [2 p. l. 624
pp.]

* The plates illustrating the first volume, and representing the anatomy of fishes, were in one edition,
issued in a folio fascicular.
† In this enumeration, I have adopted without verification the statements by Dr. Günther, published
in the several volumes (I, II, III, V, VI) of his Catalogue of Fishes, and added Pterophyllum (1 sp.),
Pomacentridae (7 sp.), Labridae (231 sp.), Cyprinidae and Cyprinodontidae (198+51–415 sp.), Esocidae
(10 sp.), Galaxiidae (7 sp.), Scombresocidae (90 sp.), Mormyridae (30 sp.), Amiidae (10 sp.), Umbridae
(1 sp.; and Salmonidae (105 sp.)

Atlas. [Pl. 1–14 to v. 1, with 2 pp. (1–8) explanatory, including title ; Pl. 15–26 to v. 2, with separate title-page and pp. 9–12 explanatory.]

The plan of this work was quite elaborate, and systematic summaries of the anatomical characterization of the various major groups have been given in the volume published. In addition to an extended introduction on Ichthyology. 618 nominal species are described or indicated, including those which the author did not especially call doubtful, but which, from want of sufficient precision and details in the descriptions or other cause, he could not contrast in his synoptical tables : these 618 species were arranged under 101 genera, 35 families, and 7 orders, and represented 4 subclasses.

In order to exhibit the contrast in the mode of treatment of the groups in question by two contemporaneous ichthyologists, the following details respecting the numbers of species are given without other comment than that the sequence and details of classification in Günther's work are also different.

	Dumeril, 1865–70.	Günther, 1870.
I°. Sous-classe, Elasmobranches		
Plagiostomes		
Squales	129 (+10 d)	128+18 d.
Raies	177 (+ 6 d)	130+37 d.
Holocephales	8	4
II°. Sous-classe, Ganoides.		
Chondrostés	85	22+10 d.
Holostés	8	
Lépidostéides	30	8+ 1 d.
Polyptérides	6	2
Amiadés	12	1
III°. Sous-classe, Dipnés	2	2
IV°. Sous-classe, Lophobranches		
Hypostomidés	4	4
Prostomidés	165	116+25 d.

1859–1870.

GÜNTHER (Albert C. L. G.). Catalogue of the fishes in the British museum. By Albert Günther, · · · · Volume first [to volume eight].—London : printed by order of the trustees. 1859–1870. [8vo., 8 v.]

This important work was commenced with a more restricted design and title, the first three volumes being designated as indicated below, and the general title was only assumed with the fourth volume ; at the end of that volume, general titles for the preceding ones were supplied, and that and all subsequent ones had double titles, —the general and the special here reproduced, viz :—

v. 1–3.—Catalogue of the Acanthopterygian fishes in the collection of the British museum. By Dr. Albert Günther.

Volume first. Gasterosteidæ, Berycidæ, Percidæ. Aphredoderidæ, Pristipomatidæ, Mullidæ, Sparidæ. · · · · 1859. [Genera title + xxxix, 524 pp.—10s.]

Volume second. Squamipinnes, Cirrhitidæ, Triglidæ, Trachinidæ, Sciænidæ, Polynemidæ, Sphyrænidæ, Trichiuridæ, Scombridæ, Carangidæ, Xiphidæ. · · · · 1860. [General title + xxi, 548 pp.—8s. 6d.]

Volume third. Gobiidæ. Discoboli, Oxudercidæ, Batrachidæ, Pediculati, Blen-
niidæ, Acanthoclinidæ, Comephoridæ, Trachypteridæ, Lophotidæ, Teuthi-
didæ, Acronuridæ, Hoplognathidæ, Malacanthidæ, Nandidæ, Polycentridæ,
Labyrinthici, Luciocephalidæ, Atherinidæ, Mugilidæ, Ophiocephalidæ, Tri-
chonotidæ, Cepolidæ, Gobiesocidæ, Psychrolutidæ, Centriscidæ, Fistulariidæ,
Mastacembelidæ, Notacanthi. . . . . 1861. [General title + xxv, 586 +
x pp.*—10s. 6d.]

v. 4.—Catalogue of the Acanthopterygii pharyngognathi and Anacanthini in the
collection of the British museum, ... 1862. [General title + xxi, 534
pp.—8s. 6d.]

v. 5.—Catalogue of the Physostomi, containing the families Siluridæ, Characi-
nidæ, Haplochitonidæ, Sternoptychidæ, Scopelidæ, Stomiatidæ in the collection
of the British museum, ... 1864. [(including general title) xxii, 455
pp.—]

v. 6.—Catalogue of the Physostomi, containing the families Salmonidæ, Percop-
sidæ, Galaxidæ, Mormyridæ, Gymnarchidæ, Esocidæ, Umbridæ, Scombresocidæ,
Cyprinodontidæ in the collection of the British museum, ... 1866. [xv,
368 pp.]

v. 7.—Catalogue of the Physostomi, containing the families Heteropygii, Cypri-
nidæ, Gonorhynchidæ, Hyodontidæ, Osteoglossidæ, Clupeidæ, Chirocentridæ,
Alepocephalidæ, Notopteridæ, Halosauridæ in the collection of the British museum, ... 1868. [xx, 512 pp.]

v. 8.—Catalogue of the Physostomi, containing the families Gymnotidæ, Sym-
branchidæ, Muraenidæ, Pegasidæ, and of the (orders) Lophobranchii, Plectognathi, [and sub-classes] Dipnoi, Ganoidei, Chondropterygii, Cyclostomata,
Leptocardii, in the British museum, ... 1870. [xxv, 549 pp.]

" In the present work, 6843 species are regarded as well established and described;
whilst 1682 others are doubtful and referred to by name only. Assuming, then, that
about one-half of the latter will be ultimately admitted into the system, and that,
since the publication of the volume of this work, about 1000 species have been
described elsewhere, we may put the total number of fishes known at present as about
9000." Gthr. v. 8, p. vi.

* A "Systematic synopsis of the families of the Acanthopterygian fishes" (x pp.) is given as an appendix to the third volume.

INDEX.